# AIR FRYE COOKBOOK FOR BEGINNERS:

*Start a Fast Track of Tasty Recipes Among Crispy & Simple Delicacies, Forgetting the Time Wasted Reheating Sad & Mushy Foods in the Microwave, Oven or Frying with Oils that Make You Heavy [II EDITION]*

## SARAH ROSLIN

# AIR FRYER COOKBOOK FOR BEGINNERS:

# CONTENTS

# CHAPTER 12

# CHAPTER 13

# INTRODUCTION

We're all far more kitchen savvy than we've ever been before. That means we want to purchase gadgets that make our cooking lives more accessible and that enhance the foods we make. Air fryers do precisely that.

Air fryers are pretty commonplace in kitchens these days. Someone might have gifted you an air fryer, or you might have seen a great deal online and bought it on a whim. Either way, you can look forward to creating delicious meals with your new gadget very quickly.

Air fryers give you a very versatile approach to cooking and have significant benefits too. When using an air fryer, you're not cooking in fat or oil; you're cooking with the air, which means most of the calorie amount of the fat you typically use isn't there. The other plus point is that cooking in the air makes your food crispier and fresher.

Did you know you can make snacks and desserts in an air fryer and regular meals? That's how versatile they are!

You'll find countless types of air fryers for sale, so you need to do your best to find the one that's right for you. That comes down to doing your research, shopping around, and reading reviews before spending your cash. Once you have purchased your chosen air fryer, you must follow the manufacturer's instructions to use it correctly. All models are slightly different, and while you can easily follow recipe instructions, how you heat and use your air fryer will be other from model to model.

However, the one thing all air fryers have in common is how easy they are to use, clean, and maintain. But, first things first, let's discuss what an air fryer is and why it's an excellent choice for you.

## What is an Air Fryer?

We've already mentioned that an air fryer is a kitchen appliance that cooks your foods in air rather than oil and fat. Cooking in an air fryer is cleaner, easier, and healthier than using a deep fat fryer. When you taste air-fried foods, you'll notice the difference. They have a really authentic, home-cooked taste to them, with a fresh crunch to everything. For the most part, you simply need to add your ingredients to your air fryer in the recipe order and follow the instructions. All air fryers are easy to use and once you understand the features on your particular model, there'll be no stopping you. It's a good idea to ensure that you keep your air fryer out on your kitchen countertop and don't use it once or twice and then store it in the cupboard. There is an 'out of sight, out of mind' problem with all kitchen appliances and you might not get the best use out of it if it's not easily accessible. By having your air fryer within easy reach, you'll be able to use it every day to create delicious breakfasts, lunches, dinners, desserts, and even snacks. It's a truly versatile machine that will surprise you with its never-ending options.

## Why is an Air Fryer a Good Choice?

You only have to do a quick online search for kitchen appliances and you'll find all manner of gadgets on sale. Some are good, some are not so good. So what sets an air fryer apart and makes it one of those things that you just have to invest in?

We've already mentioned that air fryers are easy to use and that they make your food taste great, but let's outline a list here so you can see the benefits of using an air fryer on a regular basis.

- Air fryers are very easy to use
- Different models have a range of different features
- Ideal for busy lifestyles as your food will be cooked quickly
- Foods are cooked in air, which cuts down on the amount of oil you consume daily
- Your foods will be crispier and fresher
- Streamlined versions are easy to leave on your countertop and easy to store away when necessary
- Modern appliances are easy to clean and some parts can even be washed in a dishwasher (always check your particular

appliance instructions to be sure this is the case for your model)

- A huge number of recipes can be created in your air fryer - more than you know right now!

It's vital that you do your homework when purchasing an air fryer and shop around. You'll find many different models on the market, and it pays to ensure that you're purchasing an appliance that will suit your needs.

When you're looking to buy an air fryer, these are the things you really need to keep in mind:

**Air fryer capacity** - All air fryers have a different capacity in terms of how much food you can cook inside them at any time. If you have a large family, you'll need a bigger capacity, which will probably have a larger price tag. However, if it's only 1-4 people in your household, you can probably get away with a regular-sized air fryer.

**Your budget** - Don't splurge a huge amount of cash on an air fryer with a million features you will not use. Identify your budget and find an air fryer that falls within that range.

**Different features** - Yes, you don't need an all singing, all dancing appliance, but do some research into the various features available and choose the ones that are important to you. This will inform your purchasing decision.

**Make and guarantee** - When you buy anything from a big brand name, you usually feel more confident that you're getting quality and that it will last. If this is important to you, go for a big name in the kitchen appliance world. Also, ensure you get at least a year's guarantee with your appliance, which is usually the case.

## Oil Fried Food Vs. Air Fried Foods

We know that air fryers cook your food in air, not oil, as a typical deep-fat fryer would. If you use a regular frying pan or deep fat fryer, add some heatable oil to the pan and cook the food. The issue here is that the ingredients you add to the pan or fryer soak up some of that oil, creating a different texture and, in most cases, adding to the calorie and fat content of the food you're cooking. The other problem with cooking in oil is that you need to be extremely careful, as it's easy for 'spits' of oil to fly out of the pan, burning anyone standing too close. Of course, improper supervision of oil frying can also result in fires in some cases. While frying fat foods tends to work out cheaper, the ever-rising cost of purchasing oil means that an air fryer will probably pay for itself over time. You will save on buying oil and pay for the electricity your air fryer needs to turn on and create energy. Electric isn't particularly low-cost these days either. However, modern air fryers are pretty energy efficient, and the amount of electricity this type of device uses is relatively low, especially compared to older models. For that reason, consider the energy efficiency rating when purchasing an air fryer and choose accordingly.

Oil-fried foods are unhealthier than air-fried foods. Air frying is thought to cut down on the calorie content in any meal by as much as 80% in some cases, and your food will be crispier because it's not absorbing oil. That is why air fryers are considered to be a good option for anyone who wants a fresher taste to their traditionally fried foods, e.g. French fries, without the 'soggy' and almost wet consistency that can sometimes come from frying in oil.

## Different Air Fryers on The Market Today

When deciding on which air fryer to buy, you need to know about the different types on the market. On the whole, there are two main types and the one you opt for needs to be a type that can not only fit comfortably on your kitchen countertop, but one that is also going to do exactly what you need it to do. Everyone has different needs, so be sure to think about what you want to get out of your air fryer before splashing the cash. The two main air fryers on the modern market are:

- Basket air fryer, including cylindrical basket air fryer
- Air fryer ovens

You may also hear about paddle air fryers, however these are much less popular and aren't as widely available. Bear in mind that regardless of which type of air fryer you opt for, you can still cook the same food quickly and with the same results. It's simply the pros and cons that make each one stand out. That's why it's important to understand the basic differences. Lets's take a look at each one in turn.

# Basket Air Fryer

The basket air fryer is the most common type of air fryer you'll find on the market and there are many options which are quite low in price. Within this type of air fryer, you'll also see 'cylindrical basket air fryer'. This simply refers to where the heat comes from. In this case, the air is heated at the top of the fryer and then it circulates around your food, placed in the basket. Basket air fryers have, as the name suggests, a basket inside which is removable and this is where you place your food to be cooked. However, as with any type of kitchen appliance, there are pros and cons.

## Pros:

- Basket air fryers are widely available at good prices
- These types are quite compact and therefore need much less space on your counter top
- Ingredients are easy to add the basket and you can shake them to ensure even cooking
- Basket air fryers heat up quite quickly, sometimes in as little as 2 minutes
- These air fryers hold the air in and don't make your kitchen hot

## Cons:

- Basket air fryers can be quite loud while they're cooking
- You cannot see the food while it is cooking, which means it may overcook if you don't set it properly
- Air fryers can only do one thing - cook food. There aren't as many features with basket air fryers compared to oven air fryers
- Due to the compact size, basket air fryers only fit small dishes inside
- You will need to cook your food in batches if you have a large family, as basket air fryers have less capacity

# Oven Air Fryers

The second option is an oven air fryer. This type of air fryer still cooks your food in air, therefore ensuring crispy and fresh-tasting food, but rather than having baskets inside, these types have racks inside that hold baking trays. The air is created at the top of the oven and then blown downward to cook the food. However, these types of air fryers can do more than basket air fryers, i.e. they can toast, bake, broil and even rotisserie. Let's look at the pros and cons.

## Pros:

- Several different cooking functions possible, as mentioned above
- Larger capacity. These are ideal for larger families and means you won't need to cook in batches
- The included glass door means you can see food as it is cooking
- Oven air fryers are quieter than basket air fryers
- Many different sizes of baking dishes can fit inside
- You can place your food higher or lower down in the oven, so you can control cooking time and intensity
- Depending upon the model, some parts of an oven air fryer are usually dishwasher safe

## Cons:

- Larger size means oven air fryers aren't as compact and therefore take up more space on your counter top
- Oven air fryers are typically higher in cost because of the extra features on offer
- Unlike a basket air fryer, you can't shake your food mid-way
- Oven air fryers usually make your kitchen a little hotter than basket air fryers
- May take a longer time to preheat, compared to a basket air fryer

Within each type of air fryer you will find different makes and models. Read reviews before making a purchasing choice and look closely at each type to decide which is going to suit your needs over the long-term. If you want your air fryer to complete many different cooking tasks, an oven air fryer is a better choice. However, if you don't need many features, perhaps a basket air fryer will be sufficient for you.

## The Elements of an Air Fryer

Upon shopping for an air fryer, you'll quickly see the sheer number of makes and models on the market. However, as different as they appear, they all have essential parts. Understanding how those parts work in the cooking process helps you to get to know your new appliance better.

The three essential parts that all air fryers have include:

- Inner basket
- Outer basket (including the drawer)
- Cake pan
- Heating element

Of course, the outer part of every air fryer will be slightly different. More expensive models will be larger in capacity and will have more settings, compared to lower-cost models which tend to be smaller in capacity and have more basic functions.

Let's take a more detailed look at each of the elements that make up the whole air fryer.

## Inner Basket

The inner basket is the part that holds your food and is therefore the main feature of any appliance. While your food is being cooked, it will sit side inside the basket and the air will circulate around it. Of course, that description leads you to believe that the basket will have holes around it, allowing the hot air to permeate through.

Some models also feature baskets that have holes in the bottom, and this is designed to allow excess heat to leave the basket and, therefore, not overcook your food. You may also find some particular models that feature top vents intended to do the same thing.

The holes in the inner basket also help excess fat to drip out of the bottom and into the bottom of the appliance, hence why it will need cleaning regularly. Of course, you're not adding oil to your food, as you're cooking in the air, but natural fats escape from certain ingredients and will need to drip away.

## Outer Basket/drawer

The outer basket holds the inner basket, allowing your food to cook perfectly. This is also the part of the air fryer that catches the drips of fat or any crumbs of food that fall out of the inner basket during the cooking process. However, nothing will escape from the outer basket, as this part is fully encased, with no holes.

The primary purpose of this outer basket is to allow ease of cleaning and to stop anything leaking onto your countertop. For your air fryer to turn on to cook your food, you will need to ensure that the outer basket is secured in place; most models simply won't switch on otherwise.

It's effortless to remove and insert your outer basket as it fits snugly into the air fryer outer casing and will click in place. This part of the air fryer also has a drawer that sits underneath the main inner basket, and it is here where you will notice oil and grease collecting.

## Cake Pan

Not all models have a cake pan included but you will find that many these days do. This is a part of the air fryer that is mostly used when baking, e.g. for cakes, as the name suggests. In that case, you will use this for cakes, breads, pizzas, and perhaps casseroles.

When using the cake pan, you won't use the inner basket. That is because when you're baking, you don't expect any food to drip out - however that does rely on you not overfilling your cake pan!

Cake pans often have a non-stick lining so that whatever you make is able too slide out easily and many are made of stainless steel or aluminum. However, some modern models will feature silicone cake pans.

## Heating Element

Without a doubt, the most important part of your air fryer is the heating element, something which all models need! The heating element turns the energy from the plug into heat, which then cooks your food without the need for oil.

The electric cord and plug on your air fryer will need to be kept clean and most models have a wind-around section on the back that allows you to store the cable and plug safely when your air fryer is not in use.

## Tips & Tricks of Air Fryer Use

When learning how to use your air fryer, the first few attempts will be somewhat of a 'trial and error' kind of affair. This is completely normal with any new appliance. As long as you follow the guidelines on how to use your particular model, you will achieve your desired results very quickly after starting to use your air fryer. However, there are some common tricks and tips you can use that will allow you to master your new air fryer much faster and be able to start creating delicious meals and snacks from the get-go. Here we share some of the best tricks you can use.

- All makes and models vary across different brands and it could be that your particular appliance has different temperature control settings to what you may be used to. It could be that your appliance doesn't have the exact temperature setting that you see written down in a recipe. If that's the case, the user manual should give you some advice on what temperature to go for.

- Many recipes will tell you to pre-heat your air fryer. While you can do this if you want to, it isn't necessary. Air fryers heat up extremely quickly and it will be at the desired temperature you have chosen within a few minutes at most.

- When using your air fryer, make sure that it is on a flat, even surface and allow around 5" space between the back of the fryer and any walls or other surfaces. This will allow the hot air to escape.

- When reading recipes you may see that they call for specific dishes or cake tins. You don't necessarily have to go out buying many accessories for your new device. Some models will come with a few accessories included, but if you look in your kitchen cupboards, you may already have what you need. Most dishes and pans that are oven-safe can often be used in an air fryer - they simply need to be the right size to fit inside the basket.

- Some recipes will ask you to spray your food with a little oil. You might wonder what the point is if you're going to be air frying! However, some foods simply need a very small amount of sprayed oil to help them cook better. In that case, a small spray bottle is all you need to avoid going overboard.

- You can use a "sling" made of out aluminum foil to help you insert and remove accessories from your air fryer, e.g. cake tins. This makes the process much easier and avoids any potential for burns. While the air fryer is in use, you would simply tuck the edges of the foil sling inside and remove carefully once cooled.

- If you're cooking foods that are quite fatty, e.g. sausages, it's a good idea to add a small amount of water to the removable drawer underneath the inner basket. This will remove any smoke and will stop your food becoming too hot.

- When cooking food, try and keep everything to one even layer if possible as this will make it easier to simply turn the food over at the halfway point and ensure even cooking.

- If you do need to use more than one layer of ingredients, be sure to give your basket a shake every so often, to ensure everything cooks evenly.

- Regardless of how many layers you use, never overcrowd the basket. You will not get the desired result and your food will be less than crispy. You may also find that certain parts of your food do not cook properly.

- To avoid any drips of fat from your food making its way onto your serving plate, make sure that you move the basket from the main drawer before serving your foods.
- Parchment paper sprayed with a small amount of cooking oil can be placed in the bottom of the inner basket when cooking breaded items or anything with a dough. This will prevent the food from sticking inside the basket holes or grooves.
- If you are cooking sandwiches in your air fryer, you can secure the top section of the bread with a toothpick. This will stop the air from dislodging the bread and affecting the outcome of your sandwich.

## Common Troubleshooting Solutions

An air fryer is an electrical appliance and sometimes you may encounter a few issues that make you scratch your head and wonder how to overcome them. The good news is that issues are relatively common and therefore have solutions to them. Here are a few common issues many people encounter with air frying food and how to solve them.

## If your food isn't that crispy …

Place less food inside your air fryer basket. The main issue here is overcrowding the basket, therefore not allowing the air to circulate freely and evenly during the cooking process. You should also make sure that you're not using too much sprayed oil, if the recipe asks for it.

## If you see white smoke …

You might panic if you see white smoke making its way out of the air fryer, however this is quite a common sight. It is most likely because grease and oil from the food has dripped down into the drawer below the basket and is burning slightly. To prevent this, place a small amount of water in the drawer that sits underneath the basket.

## If you see black smoke …

White smoke isn't a big issue when you're using an air fryer, but black smoke isn't the best sign. In this case, you need to switch off your appliance and take a look at the heating element. It's possible that some food has escaped onto the element and is burning on top of it. Allow everything to cool completely and clean thoroughly.

## If your air fryer will not turn off …

Modern air fryers have a safety feature which often causes people to panic and think their appliance isn't turning off! There is often a delay when the appliance starts to shut down and once you have turned off the machine, you'll probably notice that the fan is still blowing air around. This shouldn't last for more than around 25 seconds at most. Simply wait and the machine should shut down on its own.

## What Can't an Air Fryer Do?

As wonderful as an air fryer is, it does have its limitations. It isn't an appliance that can cook absolutely everything. However, you will find that as air fryers gain popularity, more and more recipes are being adapted to allow them to be cooked satisfactorily in this way. The following foods simply aren't suitable for air fryer, or should never even be attempted.

- **Foods in a wet type of batter** - Breaded foods work very well in an air fryer, however a wet type of batter simply won't cook that well in an air fryer and will probably drip away into the bottom basket before it has any chance to cook.
- **Dense cake batters** - If you're attempting to make a cake in your air fryer, you'll find some great recipes. However, doughnuts or cakes that have a dense batter of flour, sour cream, and sugar, will not work so well. In this case, the air will simply dry the batter out, not giving you the fluffy and moist outcome you desire. In this case, butter-based cake batters work better.
- **Excessively cheesy dishes** - Throughout this book you'll find recipes that contain cheese and for the most part,

cheese works very well in your air fryer. However, if you're cooking an excessively cheesy dish, you're going to notice that most of it drips out into the bottom drawer and leaves you with little in the actual basket. You need to think about moderation when it comes to air fryers and cheese.

- **Whole chickens -** While very small whole chickens can be cooked inside an air fryer, medium or large whole chickens will not cook evenly. In that case, you will find some parts of the chicken will be overcooked and dry, while others only just cooked. Of course, there is also the potential for some parts to not cook properly at all, which is a health risk.
- **Bacon -** This one isn't necessarily a no no, but it will leave you with a big mess to clean up. If you are going to cook bacon inside your air fryer, you'll need to line the basket with aluminum foil, to catch the grease. However, you will probably find that the natural fat from inside the bacon will spray out all over the sides and top of the fryer. If you have the time and patience to clean it, go ahead, but if not, it's probably best to avoid it.
- **Leafy greens -** The high speed of the air inside your air fryer is likely to make leafy greens move around too easily and as a result, they will cook very unevenly.

## How to Clean an Air Fryer

Before you start cleaning your air fryer, you'll need to refer to the manual to get a thorough overview. All makes and models will need to be cleaned slightly differently and to avoid any possible breakages, it's best to read the manual carefully before use. However, there are some general cleaning guidelines you can follow to make sure that your air fryer is clean at all times. It's vital that you never use abrasive sponges or a brush with steel wire to clean the air fryer. This will simply scratch and damage the inside. Also, never be tempted to scratch away at any stuck food with a knife or anything metal. This will also damage the inside. Instead, allow the area to soak in warm, soapy water and it should release itself, making it much easier to clean. Of course, your air fryer is electrical so never submerge the whole thing in water and always make sure that you unplug it before you start to clean. The air fryer should be completely cool before you clean. After regular use, you may find that you notice an unpleasant smell coming from your appliance and if that's the case, it's likely that a small amount of food is stuck within one of the small corners or crevices. You can easily clean this with an old toothbrush. Old crumbs can easily accumulate in small areas and cause such smells over time, so a thorough clean occasionally will prevent this from happening. Be sure to clean your air fryer after every single use. This means you need to wash the basket, pan, and tray with warm, soapy water. However, some parts are suitable to be cleaned in a dishwasher - check your user manual to be sure before doing this. If you're cleaning manually, use a soft, damp cloth to clean the inside and us a small amount of regular dish soap to clean thoroughly. Then, dry with a dry, soft cloth and ensure all parts are totally dry before reassembling. You should also make sure that you wipe down the outside of your air fryer every so often, and check the heating element occasionally to make sure oil residue isn't starting to build up. If so, a soft, damp cloth should allow you to remove build up. For a quick overview of a full clean after use, check out the steps below:

- Remove pans and baskets from your air fryer
- Wash with warm, soapy water, using a soft, non-abrasive sponge. At this point remove any grease or baked-on grime. You can soak these parts in warm, soapy water for up to 10 minutes
- Wipe the interior of the air fryer with a microfiber cloth and a small amount of dish soap. Once finished, use a clean, damp cloth to remove any soap residue
- Turn your air fryer upside down and wipe the heating element with a sponge or a damp cloth. Again, always use non-abrasive options here
- Wipe down the exterior of the air fryer with a damp cloth
- Ensure all parts are totally dry before putting the air fryer back together again.

## Looking After Your Air Fryer

An air fryer is an electrical device and like all devices of this kind, it needs to be looked after to ensure it lasts longer. Air fryers are very easy to look after and maintain and you simply need to follow the instructions included with your appliance to ensure that it lasts the test of time. However, there are some general rules of thumb you can follow to keep your appliance ticking along nicely over the long-term.

- Always clean your air fryer after you've used it and follow the instructions included with your appliance to find out how to clean it. All air fryers need to be cleaned slightly differently

- Avoid using sponges or cloths that have rough or abrasive surfaces and edges. These can scratch the inside of your appliance and cause damage. A soft cloth is just as effective and will clean your air fryer adequately
- Completely submerging your air fryer in water is a huge no-no! This is an electrical appliance and we all know that water and electric do not make a very good pairing!
- After using your air fryer, unplug the device and allow it to cool completely before cleaning
- Do not use any parts of your air fryer in the dishwasher, unless your manufacturer instructions state that you can do so
- In some cases, you'll need to take your air fryer apart to a certain degree when cleaning. Follow instructions and do not put back together again until all parts are totally dry.

As you can see, a lot of looking after an air fryer is common sense but as long as you follow instructions, you can look forward to a long and happy air fryer life-span. All that's left to do now is show you some truly delicious recipes you can start to make in your new gadget. Which one will you choose first?

# LEGEND

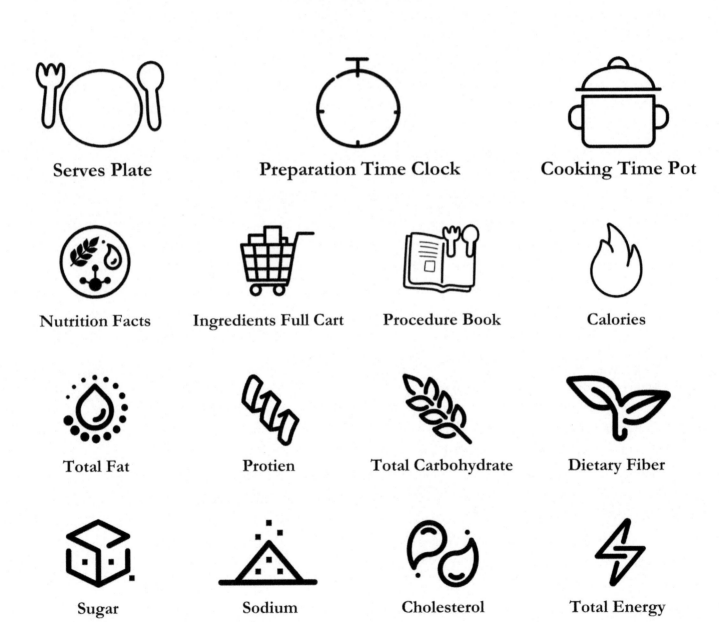

| | | |
|---|---|---|
| Serves Plate | Preparation Time Clock | Cooking Time Pot |
| Nutrition Facts | Ingredients Full Cart | Procedure Book | Calories |
| Total Fat | Protien | Total Carbohydrate | Dietary Fiber |
| Sugar | Sodium | Cholesterol | Total Energy |

# CHAPTER 1
# QUICK & EASY RECIPES

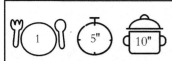 

## 1.1 French Toast

per serving · 332 Cal · 3g · 24g · 24g · 2g · 134 mg

- 2 eggs
- 5 slices of bread
- 0.5 cups of milk
- 2 tbsp flour
- 3 tbsp caster sugar
- 1 tsp cinnamon
- 1/2 tsp vanilla extract

1. Preheat your air fryer to 380°F
2. Cut your bread into three pieces
3. Combine all your ingredients in a bowl
4. Cover the bread with the mixture
5. Take a piece of parchment paper and lay it inside the air fryer
6. Arrange the bread on the parchment paper
7. Cook for 5 minutes on each side

## 1.2 Air Fryer Eggs

per serving · 300 Cal · 2g · 15g · 5g · 1g · 13 mg

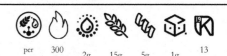

- 4 eggs
- 4oz cheese, cut into pieces
- Salt and pepper
- 2 greased ramekin dishes

1. Crack two eggs into one dish
2. Add some cheese to each dish
3. Season to your liking
4. Place in the air fryer and cook for 15 minutes at 350°F for 15 minutes

# 1.3 Easy Pancakes

| per serving | 250 Cal | 2g | 20g | 4g | 2g | 45 mg |

- 3 eggs
- 4oz plain flour
- 0.5 cups of milk
- 2 tbsp apple sauce
- 5 greased ramekin dishes

1. Preheat your air fryer to 300°F
2. Blend all your ingredients until smooth
3. Transfer the batter into the ramekin dishes
4. Fry for 8 minutes
5. Serve with any topping you desire

# 1.4. Morning Wraps

| per serving | 450 Cal | 3g | 21g | 7g | 3g | 50 mg |

- 2 corn tortillas, crushed
- 2 eggs
- 2 flour tortillas
- 1 jalapeño pepper, cut into slices
- 1 thinly sliced avocado
- 4 tbsp ranchero sauce
- 0.8 oz pinto beans, cooked

1. Add the eggs, jalapeño, sauce, the corn tortillas, the avocado, and the pinto beans to the flour tortillas
2. Fold up your wrap and put inside the air fryer
3. Cook at 300°F for 6 minutes

# 1.5 Cheese & Ham in Puff Pastry

| per serving | 450 Cal | 5g | 21g | 8g | 2g | 65 mg |

- 4 large eggs
- 1 piece of puff pastry
- 4 tbsp cheddar cheese, grated
- 4 slices of ham, chopped

1. Cut your pastry into four equal pieces
2. Cook two pieces of the pastry inside the air fryer for 8 minutes at 390°F
3. Make a hole in the middle of the cooked pastry
4. Add some cheese and ham into the middle, along with one egg
5. Cook for another 6 minutes
6. Repeat the process with your remaining ingredients

# 1.6 "Spanish" Frittata

| per serving | 460 Cal | 4g | 30g | 8g | 2g | 45 mg |

- 1 tbsp olive oil
- 3 eggs
- 1 chorizo sausage, sliced
- 1 boiled potato, cut into pieces
- 1.7 oz feta cheese, crumbled
- 1.7 oz sweetcorn
- Salt for seasoning

1. Coat your frying basket in oil and add the chorizo, potato, and corn
2. Cook at 350°F until the sausage has browned
3. Beat together the eggs with the salt and transfer to the pan
4. Add the feta and cook for 5 minutes

## 1.7 Ham & Egg Bites

| per serving | 450 Cal | 2g | 28g | 8g | 4g | 67 mg |

- 8 slices of bread, toasted
- 4 large eggs
- 2 slices of ham
- Salt and pepper
- 4 greased ramekin dishes

1. Roll out each piece of toast with a rolling pan
2. Place inside the ramekin dishes
3. Add ham around the bread
4. Crack one egg into each dish and season
5. Cook at 300°F for 15 minutes

## 1.8 Vegetable Hash Browns

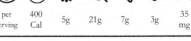

| per serving | 400 Cal | 5g | 21g | 7g | 3g | 35 mg |

- 2 tbsp olive oil
- 4 potatoes, grated and the excess water squeezed out
- 1 chopped onion
- 1 red pepper, chopped
- 1 green pepper, chopped
- 2 tbsp bicarbonate of soda
- 1 tsp cayenne pepper
- Salt and pepper

1. Place the potatoes in a large bowl of water with the bicarbonate of soda. Leave to soak for 30 minutes
2. Pat the potatoes dry and place into a bowl
3. Add the spices and oil, combining everything well
4. Cook for 10 minutes at 350°F
5. Add the other vegetables and cook for another 10 minutes

# 1.9 Air Fryer Omelette

per serving | 280 Cal | 5g | 29g | 8g | 3g | 30 mg

**Ingredients**

- 2 eggs
- 0.2 cups of milk
- 2 oz grated cheese
- Salt

**Instructions**

1. Combine the eggs and milk with a little salt
2. Grease a medium cooking pan and transfer the mixture inside
3. Place the pan inside the fryer and cook for 10 minutes at 300°F
4. Add the cheese just before the omelette has finished and cook for another 2 minutes

# 1.10 Full & Healthy Peppers

per serving | 450 Cal | 2g | 21g | 7g | 3g | 50 mg

**Ingredients**

- 2 tbsp olive oil
- 4 eggs
- 1 large bell pepper, top cut off and seeds removed
- Salt and pepper to taste

**Instructions**

1. Rub the oil over the peppers and crack one egg into each
2. Arrange the peppers inside the air fryer basket and cook for 13 minutes at 350°F
3. Season before serving

## 1.11 Sausage Surprise

per serving | 470 Cal | 9g | 35g | 10g | 3.5g | 65 mg

- 8 chopped sausages
- 2 slices of cheese, chopped
- 1 piece of pizza dough

1. Roll the pizza dough out and cut into two pieces
2. Add a little sausage and then a little cheese to the dough
3. Roll and create a triangle shape
4. Cook for 3 minutes at 370°F
5. Repeat with the other piece of dough

## 1.12 Cheesy Toast

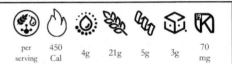

per serving | 450 Cal | 4g | 21g | 5g | 3g | 70 mg

- 1 tbsp butter, melted
- 4 slices bread
- 2 slices of cheese that melts easily
- 5 slices bacon, already cooked

1. Spread the butter onto the bread and place in the air fryer
2. Add the cheese and bacon
3. Add the other slice of bread on top
4. Cook for 4 minutes at 360°F
5. Turn the toast over and cook for a further 3 minutes

# 1.13 Breakfast Sandwich

per serving | 300 Cal | 7g | 22g | 6g | 3g | 120 mg

- 1 egg
- 1 tsp butter, melted
- 2 slices of sandwich bread
- 1/4 tsp vanilla extract
- 4 slices of cheese that melts easily
- 4 slices of ham, sliced
- 4 slices of turkey, sliced

1. Combine the egg and vanilla
2. Make a sandwich with the bread, cheese, meats and top with the other slice of bread
3. Coat the sandwich in butter and dip in the egg mixture
4. Cook for 10 minute at 390°F
5. Turn over and cook for a further 8 minutes

# 1.14 Quick Morning Doughnuts

per serving | 332 Cal | 3g | 24g | 6g | 6g | 150 mg

- 1 packet of pizza-style dough
- 1 tbsp butter, melted
- 5 tbsp jam
- 5 tbsp sugar

1. Cook the dough in the air fryer for 5 minutes at 390°F
2. Dip the cooked doughnuts in the sugar and coat completely
3. Pipe the jam inside the doughnuts

# 1.15 Spinach & Eggs

per serving | 350 Cal | 3g | 21g | 8g | 9g | 800 mg

- 1 tbsp olive oil
- 17 oz fresh spinach, wilted
- 7 oz sliced deli ham
- 4 tsp milk
- 4 eggs
- Salt and pepper
- 4 ramekin dishes, greased with butter

1. Preheat the air fryer to 340°F

2. Add the wilted spinach, ham, a quarter of the milk, and 1 egg into each dish and season

3. Cook for 20 minutes

4. Cool before consumption

# 1.16 Breakfast Pockets

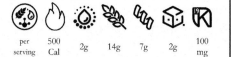

per serving | 500 Cal | 2g | 14g | 7g | 2g | 100 mg

- 5 medium eggs
- 1 pack puff pastry
- 4 cooked sausages, chopped
- 1.7 oz bacon, cooked
- 1.7 oz grated cheese

1. Scramble your eggs in a pan and halfway through, add the bacon and sausage

2. Cut your paste into rectangles

3. Add some of the mixture to half the pastry and fold over

4. Seal the edges with a fork and cook in your air fryer for 10 minutes at 360°F

# 1.17 Easy Boiled Eggs

| per serving | 400 Cal | 2g | 21g | 8g | 3g | 35 mg |

- 4 eggs
- 1 tsp cayenne pepper
- Salt and pepper

1. Preheat the air fryer to 220C

2. Place the eggs inside the fryer and cook for 15 minutes at 390°F

3. Place the eggs in ice cold water and leave to cool for 5 minutes

4. Cut the eggs and season with the spices

# 1.18 Paprika Hash

| per serving | 650 Cal | 2g | 28g | 8g | 4g | 500 mg |

- 2 tbsp olive oil
- 2 sliced of chopped bacon
- 2 potatoes, cubed
- 1 tbsp smoked paprika
- Salt and pepper

1. Preheat your air fryer to 380°F

2. Combine the oil, potatoes, bacon and seasonings

3. Place in the fryer and cook for 16 minutes, stirring regularly

# 1.19 Egg "Sandwiches"

per serving | 332 Cal | 3g | 24g | 6g | 10g | 200 mg

- Salt and pepper
- 2 eggs
- 2 slices of bread

1. Create a hole in the middle of your bread and crack an egg into each one
2. Season and place in the air fryer, cooking for 5 minutes at 350°F
3. Turn over and cook for another 2 minutes
4. Repeat with the other slice of bread

# 1.20 Creamy Breakfast Treats

per serving | 450 Cal | 3g | 20g | 8g | 3g | 350 mg

- 1 medium egg
- 1 tbsp milk
- 2 slices of bread
- 1 tbsp soft cream cheese
- 1 tbsp jam

1. Take one slice of the bread and add some jam into the middle
2. Take the other slice and add the cream cheese
3. Spread both across the edges
4. Whisk the eggs and the milk together
5. Set your fryer to 370°F
6. Dip your sandwich into the egg and place in the fryer basket
7. Cook for 5 minutes, turn and cook for another 2 minutes

# CHAPTER 2
# FISH & SEAFOOD RECIPES

## 2.1 Shrimp Pops

| per serving | 332 Cal | 3g | 24g | 6g | 10g | 250 mg |
|---|---|---|---|---|---|---|

- 10 oz shrimp pieces, popcorn shrimp will work well
- 1 tsp cayenne pepper
- Salt and pepper

1. Place the shrimp inside the air fryer and cook for 6 minutes at 370°F
2. Shake after 3 minutes
3. Season to your liking before serving

---

## 2.2 Crab Stuffed Mushrooms

| per serving | 500 Cal | 5g | 21g | 8g | 2g | 260 mg |
|---|---|---|---|---|---|---|

- 10 oz crab
- 1 egg
- 17 oz mushrooms
- Half a red onion, chopped
- 2 celery sticks, diced
- 1.2 oz seasoned breadcrumbs
- 1.7 oz grated cheese
- 1 tsp oregano
- 1 tsp hot sauce

1. Preheat your air fryer to 370°F
2. Place a piece of parchment inside your air fryer and spray with a small amount of cooking oil
3. Arrange the mushrooms with the tops facing down
4. Combine onions, celery, breadcrumbs, egg, crab, most of the cheese, oregano, and hot sauce
5. Place the mixture inside the mushrooms and sprinkle the rest of the cheese on top
6. Cook for 18 minutes

# 2.3 Zingy Shrimp

per serving | 400 Cal | 19g | 24g | 6g | 3g | 250 mg

- 1 tbsp olive oil
- 10 oz shrimp
- 1 the juice of 1 lemon
- 0.25 tsp garlic powder
- 0.25 tsp paprika
- 1 lemon, sliced
- 1 tsp pepper

1. Heat your air fryer to 390°F
2. Combine the lemon juice, pepper, garlic powder, paprika, and the olive oil
3. Coat the shrimp with the mixture and place in the air fryer
4. Cook for 8 minutes

# 2.4 Easy Breadcrumbed Fish

per serving | 600 Cal | 20g | 22g | 8g | 3g | 280 mg

- 4 tbsp olive oil
- 1 egg, beaten
- 7 oz breadcrumbs
- 4 fillets of fish

1. Heat your air fryer to 320°F
2. Combine the olive oil and the breadcrumbs
3. Dip the fish in the egg, breadcrumbs and place inside the air fryer
4. Cook for 12 minutes

## 2.5 Asian Fish Patties

| per serving | 553 Cal | 3g | 29g | 6g | 1g | 380 mg |

- 1 oz breadcrumbs
- 1 can of salmon, drained
- 2 eggs
- 0.25 tsp salt
- 1. 5 tbsp Thai red curry paste
- 1.5 tbsp brown sugar
- Zest of 1 lime

1. Combine all ingredients together
2. Create patties that are around 1" thick
3. Cook the patties in the air fryer at 310°F for 4 minutes on each side

## 2.6 Simple Fish Fingers

| per serving | 655 Cal | 12g | 30g | 6g | 1g | 390 mg |

- Dressing: Salt and pepper, 1 tsp mixed herbs, 1 tsp thyme
- 1 tsp parsley
- The juice of 1 small lemon
- 1 fish fillet
- 1.7 oz flour
- 1 egg, beaten
- 2 slices bread, grated and seasoned

1. Preheat your air fryer to 320°F
2. Combine the fish, seasonings, lemon juice and mixed herbs in a blender
3. Create finger shapes out of the mixture
4. First dip in the flour, then the egg, and finally the breadcrumbs
5. Cook for 8 minutes

## 2.7 Salmon Burgers

| per serving | 590 Cal | 10g | 31g | 6g | 2g | 360 mg |

- 1 egg
- 14 oz salmon
- 1 onion, diced
- 7 oz breadcrumbs
- 1 tsp dill weed

1. Combine the egg, onion, dill weed, salmon and breadcrumbs
2. Create burger shapes and place into the air fryer
3. Cook for 5 minutes at 300°F
4. Turn and cook for another 5 minutes

## 2.8 Spicy Shrimp Boil

| per serving | 450 Cal | 9g | 21g | 6g | 1g | 360 mg |

- 10 oz shrimp, cooked
- 14 pieces of sausage
- 5 parboiled potatoes, halved
- 4 small corn on the cobs, cut into pieces
- 1 onion, diced
- 3 tbsp old bay seasoning

1. Combine all ingredients
2. Line the air fryer with foil
3. Cook at 390°F for 6 minutes
4. Stir and cook for another 6 minutes

# 2.9 Fish Taco Bowls

per serving | 600 Cal | 23g | 24g | 6g | 3g | 380 mg

- 14 oz fish cut into pieces
- 10 oz cauliflower rice
- 1 avocado, sliced
- 1 tsp chilli powder
- ½ tsp paprika
- 0.8 oz pickled red onions
- 0.8 oz sour cream
- ½ tsp cumin
- 1 tbsp lime juice
- 0.8 oz fresh coriander
- 1 tbsp sriracha

1. Season the fish with the spices

2. Cook the fish in the air fryer at 390°F for about 12 minutes

3. Meanwhile, cook the cauliflower rice according to instructions and add the coriander and lime juice once cooked

4. Divide the mixture between your serving bowls along with the fish, red onions and avocado

5. Drizzle the sriracha and sour cream on top

---

# 2.10 Air Fryer Scallops

per serving | 500 Cal | 9g | 21g | 7g | 2g | 380 mg

- Dressings: pepper and salt
- 1 tbsp olive oil
- 6 scallops

1. Brush the fillets with olive oil and season

2. Place in the air fryer and cook at 380°F for 2 mins

3. Turn and cook for another 2 minutes

## 2.11 Air Fryer Mussels

- 1 tbsp butter
- 14 oz mussels, cleaned and soaked for half an hour
- 0.8 cups of water
- 1 tsp basil
- 1 tsp parsley
- 2 tsp minced garlic
- 1 tsp chives

1. Place all ingredients inside the air fryer and set to 350°F
2. Cook for 3 minutes
3. If the mussels haven't opened, cook for a further 2 minutes

## 2.12 Boozy Fish Tacos

- Dressings: Salt and pepper, 1 tbsp cumin, ½ tsp chilli powder
- 2 soft corn tortillas
- 10 oz plain flour
- 10 oz cornstarch
- 1 can of beer
- 2 eggs

1. Combine the eggs and beer
2. Separately, combine the cornstarch, chilli powder, flour, cumin, and salt and pepper
3. Dip the fish in the egg mixture then the flour mixture
4. Set your fryer to 360°F and cook for 15 minutes
5. Serve in the tortillas

# 2.13 Herby Tilapia

| per serving | 650 Cal | 19g | 24g | 9g | 2g | 260 mg |
|---|---|---|---|---|---|---|

- Dressings: salt and pepper, 2 tsp olive oil, 2 tsp fresh parsley (chopped), 2 tsp fresh chives (chopped), 1 tsp garlic, minced
- tilapia fillets

1. Preheat your air fryer to 390°F
2. Combine the olive oil with the chives, garlic, parsley, and seasoning
3. Coat the fish fillets
4. Place the fish into the air fryer and cook for 10 minutes

---

# 2.14 Tartar Battered Fish Sticks

| per serving | 690 Cal | 19g | 31g | 13g | 3g | 300 mg |
|---|---|---|---|---|---|---|

- 14 oz cod fillets, sliced
- 6 tbsp mayonnaise
- 2 tbsp dill pickle
- 1 tsp seafood seasoning
- 10.5 oz breadcrumbs

1. Preheat the air fryer to 380°F
2. Combine the mayonnaise, seafood seasoning, and dill pickle
3. Add the fish and coat
4. Dip the fish in the breadcrumbs and place in the air fryer
5. Cook for 12 minutes

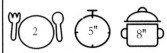 

## 2.15 Coconut Shrimp

per serving 630 Cal 19g 30g 13g 2g 360 mg

- 10.5 oz raw shrimp
- 8 oz flour
- 4 tbsp honey
- 2 eggs
- 5 oz flaked coconut
- 1 Serrano chilli, sliced
- 0.8 oz breadcrumbs
- 0.2 cups of lime juice
- Salt and pepper

1. Combine the flour and pepper
2. Separately, beat the eggs
3. In another bowl mix breadcrumbs and coconut
4. Dip each of the shrimp in the flour mix then the egg and then cover in the breadcrumbs
5. Place in the air fryer and cook at 390°F for 6-8 mins
6. Turn halfway through
7. Combine the honey, lime juice, and chilli to serve

# CHAPTER 3
# VEGETARIAN PLATE RECIPES

## 3.1 Aubergine Parmesan

| per serving | 690 Cal | 19g | 31g | 13g | 3g | 230 mg |

- Dressings: Salt and pepper, 1 tsp Italian seasoning
- 3 tbsp whole wheat flour
- 3 tbsp Parmesan cheese, grated
- 1 egg
- 1 aubergine, halved
- 4 slices of bread, grated
- 1 tbsp water
- 5 tbsp marinara sauce
- 1 oz grated cheese

1. Add a little salt to both sides of the aubergine
2. Combine the egg, flour, and water
3. Take a plate and add the breadcrumbs, parmesan, and Italian seasoning, combining well
4. Dip the aubergine into the egg mixture and the breadcrumbs
5. Preheat the air fryer to 390°F and place the aubergine inside
6. Cook for 8 minutes
7. Add the marinara sauce and mozzarella on top and cook for another 2 minutes

---

## 3.2 Air Fryer Ravioli

| per serving | 456 Cal | 11g | 15g | 11g | 2g | 240 mg |

- 1 pack of ravioli
- 1 tbsp olive oil
- 0.8 cups of buttermilk
- 7 oz breadcrumbs
- 5 tbsp marinara sauce
- Salt and pepper

1. Preheat the air fryer to 380°F
2. Place the buttermilk in a bowl and place the breadcrumbs in another bowl
3. Dip each piece of ravioli in the buttermilk and then the breadcrumbs
4. Place in the air fryer and cook for 7 minutes
5. Add some oil if the ravioli becomes dry
6. Serve with the marinara sauce

# 3.3 Citrus Cauliflower

| per serving | 550 Cal | 21g | 30g | 13g | 1g | 250 mg |

- 1 cauliflower, separated into florets
- 2 tsp olive oil
- 0.8 cups of water
- 7 oz plain flour
- 2 garlic cloves, minced
- 1 tsp ginger, minced
- 0.6 cups of orange juice
- 3 tbsp white vinegar
- 1/2 tsp red pepper flakes
- 1 tsp sesame oil
- 3.5 oz brown sugar
- 3 tbsp soy sauce
- 1 tbsp cornstarch
- Salt and pepper

1. Combine the water, salt, and flour
2. Dip each floret of cauliflower into the mixture
3. Arrange in the air fryer and cook for 15 minutes at 380°F
4. Combine the rest of the ingredients in a saucepan and bring to a simmer for 3 minutes
5. Drizzle the sauce over the cauliflower

# 3.4 Cheese Tikka

| per serving | 690 Cal | 19g | 31g | 13g | 3g | 280 mg |

- 8 metal skewers
- 1 onion, chopped
- 1 yellow pepper, chopped
- 1 red pepper, chopped
- 1 green pepper, chopped
- 2 tbsp chopped coriander
- The juice of 1 lemon
- 1 tbsp dried fenugreek leaves
- 1 tsp turmeric powder
- 1 tsp garam masala
- 1 tsp red chilli powder
- 1 tsp ginger garlic paste
- 0.8 cups of yogurt
- 1 tbsp olive oil
- 8.8 oz paneer cheese, cubed

1. Combine the yogurt, garlic paste, red chilli powder, garam masala, turmeric powder, lemon juice, fenugreek, and chopped coriander
2. Add the cheese and coat well. Leave in the refrigerator for 2 hours
3. Take your skewers and add the cheese, peppers, and onions alternately
4. Add a little oil and place in the air fryer
5. Cook for 3 minutes at 390°F
6. Turn and cook for 3 more minutes

**2** | **5"** | **8"**

# 3.5 Falafel Patties

per serving | 445 Cal | 10g | 19g | 12g | 1g | 580 mg

- Dressings:Salt and pepper, 1 tbsp parsley, 1 tbsp oregano, 1 tbsp coriander, 1 tbsp garlic puree
- 4 tbsp soft cheese
- 3 tbsp Greek yogurt
- 1 oz feta cheese
- 1 oz cheese, grated
- 1 lemon
- 1 onion
- 5 oz oats
- 1 can of chickpeas

1. Blend the chickpeas, onion, lemon rind, garlic, and seasonings
2. Add the mixture to a bowl and add half the soft cheese, cheese, and the feta
3. Create patties with your hands and roll in the oats
4. Cook at 370°F for 8 minutes
5. Combine the rest of the soft cheese, greek yogurt, and lemon juice in a bowl for the serving sauce

---

   **2** | **5"** | **15"**

# 3.6 Mushroom Pasta

per serving | 450 Cal | 19g | 31g | 13g | 3g | 280 mg

- 8 oz mushrooms, sliced
- 7 oz cooked pasta
- 1 onion, chopped
- 2 tsp garlic, minced
- 1 tsp salt
- ½ tsp red pepper flakes
- 2.6 oz cup double cream
- 2.4 oz mascarpone cheese
- 1 tsp dried thyme
- 1 tsp ground black pepper

1. Place all the ingredients in a bowl and mix well
2. Heat the air fryer to 320°F
3. Grease a 7x3 inch pan and pour in the mixture
4. Place in the air fryer and cook for 15 minutes stirring halfway through
5. Pour over your cooked pasta

# 3.7 Courgette Rolls

- 14 oz oats
- 1.4 oz feta, crumbled
- 1 egg, beaten
- 5 oz courgette, grated
- 1 tsp lemon rind
- 6 basil leaves, thinly sliced
- 1 tsp oregano
- 1 tsp dill
- Salt and pepper

1. Place all ingredients in a bowl, except for the oats
2. Blend the oats until coarse
3. Add the oats and combine
4. Form into balls and place in the air fryer
5. Cook for 10 minutes at 390°F

# 3.8 Cheese & Pasta Quiche

- 1 packet of ready shortcrust pastry
- 8 tbsp pasta
- 2 eggs
- 14 oz grated cheese
- 2 tbsp Greek yogurt
- 0.6 cups of milk
- 1 tsp garlic puree
- 4 greased ramekin dishes

1. Line the ramekin dishes with the shortcrust pastry
2. Combine the yogurt, garlic, and macaroni
3. Spoon into the dishes until almost full
4. Mix the egg and milk together and pour over the pasta
5. Add the cheese and place in the air fryer
6. Cook at 370°F for 20 minutes

# 3.9 Lentil Balls

| per serving | 500 Cal | 19g | 18g | 13g | 1g | 360 mg |

- 2 cans lentils
- 7 oz rice
- 1.6 cups of water
- 7 oz walnut halves
- 3 tbsp dried mushrooms
- 3 tbsp parsley
- 1.5 tbsp tomato paste
- 3.5 oz bread crumbs
- 2 tbsp lemon juice and zest
- Salt and pepper

1. Blend the lentils, walnuts, mushrooms, parsley, tomato paste, salt, pepper in a food processor
2. Fold in the bread crumbs
3. Create small balls and place in the air fryer at 380°F
4. Cook for 10 minutes
5. Turn and cook for a further 5 minutes
6. Add the rice to a pan with water. Bring the mixture to the boil and turn down to a simmer for 20 minutes.
7. Add the lemon juice, lemon zest, and salt

# 3.10 Air Fryer Vegetable Bake

| per serving | 400 Cal | 19g | 31g | 13g | 3g | 230 mg |

- 1 oz plain flour
- 10 oz packet vegetable bake

1. Preheat the air fryer to 380°F
2. Mix the flour with the vegetable bake
3. Create ball shapes and arrange in the fryer
4. Cook for 10 minutes

# 3.11 Mediterranean Gnocchi

per serving | 590 Cal | 21g | 35g | 6g | 2g | 180 mg

- 1 packet of prepared gnocchi
- 2 tbsp olive oil
- 5 oz cherry tomatoes, cut into halves
- 2 tbsp balsamic vinegar
- 3 cloves of garlic, pressed
- 7 oz basil, chopped
- 7 oz mini mozzarella balls
- Salt and pepper

1. Combine the cherry tomatoes, gnocchi, oil, balsamic vinegar, garlic, and seasoning
2. Transfer to the air fryer basket and cook for 10 minutes at 390°F
3. Once cooked, transfer everything to a large mixing bowl and add the mozzarella and basil

# 3.12 Healthy Vegetarian Pizza

per serving | 390 Cal | 6g | 10g | 6g | 1g | 180 mg

- 2 wholewheat pitta breads
- 3.5 oz marinara sauce
- 7 oz baby spinach
- 1 tomato, sliced
- 1 clove garlic, sliced
- 14 oz grated cheese

1. Spread the marinara over each of the pittas
2. Sprinkle with cheese, top with spinach, plum tomato, and garlic
3. Place in the air fryer and cook for about 4 mins at 360°F

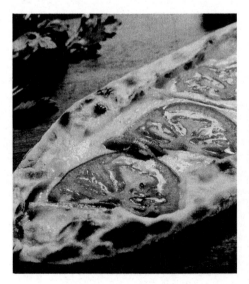

# 3.13 Air Fryer Tofu

| per serving | 200 Cal | 3g | 3g | 6g | 1g | 120 mg |

- 10 oz quinoa
- 1 block of tofu, cubed
- 1 grated carrot
- 1 sliced avocado
- 1 onion, chopped
- 0.2 cups of soy sauce
- 2 tbsp sesame oil
- 1 tsp garlic powder
- 2 tbsp Tahini dressing
- 3 bunches baby bok choy, chopped
- 1 sliced cucumber

1. Mix the soy sauce, 1 tbsp sesame oil, and garlic powder together
2. Add the tofu and place to one side for 10 minutes
3. Place in the air fryer and cook at 390°F for 20 minutes - turning halfway
4. Heat the remaining sesame oil in a pan and cook the onions for about 4 minutes
5. Add the bok choy and cook for another 4 minutes
6. Divide the quinoa between your bowls add bok choy, carrot, cucumber, and avocado.
7. Top with the tofu
8. Drizzle with Tahini

---

# 3.14 Creamy Pasta Bake

| per serving | 450 Cal | 18g | 15g | 11g | 1g | 210 mg |

- 5 oz pasta - any type you like
- 400g grated cheese
- 2 tbsp Greek yogurt
- 2 eggs
- 0.6 cups of milk
- 1 tsp garlic puree
- 4 greased ramekin dishes

1. Rub the inside of 4 ramekins with flour
2. Mix the yogurt, garlic, and pasta together and place inside the ramekins
3. Mix the egg and milk together
4. Divide between the ramekins and top with cheese
5. Cook in the air fryer at 370°F for 20 minutes

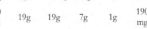

- 0.5 cups of coconut cream
- 1.7 oz cheese, grated
- 2 potatoes, sliced thinly
- 2 eggs, beaten
- 1 tbsp plain flour
- 4 greased ramekin dishes

1. Place the potatoes in the air fryer, and cook for 10 minutes at 360°F
2. Combine the eggs, coconut cream, and flour
3. Line four ramekins with the potato slices
4. Add the cream mixture
5. Sprinkle with cheese, and cook for 10 minutes at 390°F

# CHAPTER 4
# VEGAN PLATE RECIPES

## 4.1 Artichoke & Pumpkin Seed Pasta

| per serving | 400 Cal | 5g | 6g | 4g | 1g | 700 mg |

- 3.5 oz pasta - your choice
- 6 artichoke hearts
- 2 tbsp pumpkin seeds
- 1 can of chickpeas
- 1.7 oz basil leaves
- 2 tbsp lemon juice
- 1 clove garlic
- 0.5 tsp miso paste
- 1 tsp olive oil

1. Cook the chickpeas in the air fryer at 390°F for 12 minutes
2. Meanwhile, cook your pasta on the stove to your liking and place in serving bowls
3. Add the remaining ingredients to a food processor and blend
4. Top the pasta with the pesto mix and roasted chickpeas

## 4.2 Jackfruit Taquitos

| per serving | 380 Cal | 7g | 4g | 7g | 1g | 300 mg |

- 1 Jackfruit
- 4 wheat tortillas
- 0.2 cups of water
- 8 oz red beans
- 3.5 oz pico de gallo sauce

1. Place the jackfruit, red beans, sauce, and water in a saucepan
2. Bring to the boil and simmer for 25 minutes
3. Mash the jackfruit mixture, add ¼ cup of the mix to each tortilla, and roll up tightly
4. Spray with olive oil and place in the air fryer
5. Cook for 8 minutes at 350°F

## 4.3 Air Fryer Pierogies

- 1 tbsp olive oil
- 14 pierogies
- 1 onion, sliced
- 1 tsp sugar

1. Bring a saucepan of water to the boil and cook the pierogis for 5 minutes
2. Drain and place to one side
3. Add a little oil to the basket and add the onion, cooking for 12 minutes at 390°F
4. After 5 minutes have passed, add the sugar
5. Remove the onions and place to one side
6. Add the dumplings to the air fryer and cook for 4 minutes
7. Mix the dumplings with the onions before serving

## 4.4 Radish Browns

- Dressings: Salt and pepper, ½ tsp paprika, 1 tsp onion powder
- 1 onion, chopped
- 1 tsp coconut oil
- 10 oz radish, trimmed and chopped

1. Place the onions and radish in a bowl with the coconut oil and combine
2. Place in the air fryer and cook at 360°F for 8 minutes, shaking halfway through
3. Add seasoning and cook for another 5 minutes

2 | 5" | 35"

# 4.5 Lentil & Cabbage Patties

per serving | 400 Cal | 3g | 15g | 9g | 1g | 170 mg

- 3.5 oz black lentils
- 3.5 oz white cabbage
- 1 carrot, grated
- 1 onion, diced ad blended
- 10.5 oz oats
- 1 tbsp garlic puree
- 1 tsp cumin
- Salt and pepper

1. Cook the lentils in a pan with water for 45 minutes
2. Combine all ingredients in a bowl and use your hands to create burgers
3. Place in the air fryer and cook at 180°C for 30 minutes

2 | 5" | 12"

# 4.6 Courgette & Coriander Burgers

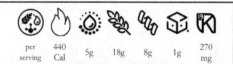

per serving | 440 Cal | 5g | 18g | 8g | 1g | 270 mg

- Dressings: Salt and pepper, 1 tsp chilli powder, 1 tsp mixed spice, 3 tbsp coriander, 1 tsp cumin
- 1 courgette, grated
- 3 spring onions, sliced
- 1 can of chickpeas, drained

1. Take a large bowl and combine the grated courgette, drained chickpeas and the sliced spring onions
2. Season to your liking and use your hands to create burgers
3. Cook in the air fryer for 12 minutes at 390°F

# 4.7 Vegan Cheese With Bread Sticks

| per serving | 490 Cal | 15g | 19g | 11g | 2g | 190 mg |

- 2 slices of bread
- 1 piece of your favorite vegan cheese
- 1 tbsp mustard

1. Cook the cheese in the air fryer for 15 minutes at 370°F
2. Meanwhile, toast your bread and cut into stripes
3. Place the cheese on top of the bread and serve with the mustard

---

# 4.8 Canarian Potatoes

| per serving | 390 Cal | 14g | 20g | 7g | 2g | 390 mg |

- 1 tbsp olive oil
- 4 potatoes, cut into wedges
- 1 tsp taco seasoning
- 2 tsp paprika
- 2 tsp dried garlic
- Salt and pepper

1. Place the potatoes and olive oil in a bowl with the seasoning and combine
2. Add to the air fryer and cook at 370°F for 20 minutes
3. Shake and turn the air fryer up to 200°C. Cook for another 3 minutes

## 4.9 Cheesy Bagel Pizza

per serving | 690 Cal | 19g | 31g | 30g | 3g | 190 mg

- 1 uncooked bagel, cut in half
- 6 slices of vegan pepperoni
- 2 slices of your favorite vegan cheese
- 2 tbsp marinara sauce
- Pinch of basil

1. Toast the bagel at 370°F for 2 minutes in the air fryer
2. Add the marinara sauce, pepperoni, and cheese
3. Return to the air fryer and cook for 5 minutes
4. Sprinkle with basil

## 4.10 Pumpkin & Lemon Pasta

per serving | 500 Cal | 15g | 14g | 6g | 1g | 680 mg

- 3.5 oz pasta of your choice
- 1.7 oz basil leaves
- 2 tbsp pumpkin seeds
- 2 tbsp lemon juice
- 1 clove garlic

1. Cook the pasta according to packet instructions
2. Add the remaining ingredients to a food processor and blend
3. Add the pasta the mixture and place in the air fryer for 5 minutes at 370°F

# 4.11 Crostini With Artichoke

per serving | 440 Cal | 10g | 3g | 9g | 2g | 190 mg

- 1 tbsp olive oil
- 1 baguette, cut into slices
- 7 oz artichoke hearts, grilled
- 3.5 oz cashews
- 1 tbsp lemon juice
- 1 tsp balsamic vinegar
- 0.5 tsp basil
- 1 clove garlic, minced
- Salt and pepper

1. Combine cashews, olive oil, lemon juice, balsamic vinegar, basil oregano, onion powder, garlic, and salt in a bowl. Set aside
2. Place the baguette slices in the air fryer and cook at 370°F for 3-4 minutes
3. Sprinkle the baguette slices with cashew mix then add the artichoke hearts

---

# 4.12 Cheesy Baked Potato

per serving | 600 Cal | 19g | 31g | 13g | 2g | 250 mg

- 1 baking potato
- 1 tsp oil
- 0.25 tsp onion powder
- 1 tbsp of vegan butter
- 1 tbsp of vegan cream cheese
- 1 tbsp olives
- 1 tbsp chives
- Salt and pepper

1. Stab the potato with a fork and rub a little oil around the edges. Season with salt and onion powder
2. Place in the air fryer and cook at 390°F for 40 minutes
3. Combine all other ingredients in a bowl and serve on top of the potato once cooked

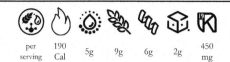
# 4.13 BBQ Soy Curls

- 1 cup of water
- 7 oz soy curls
- 1.4 oz BBQ sauce
- 1 tsp vegetable bouillon

1. Soak the soy curls in water and bouillon for 10 minutes before shredding
2. Cook in the air fryer for 3 minutes at 390°F
3. Remove from the air fryer and coat in bbq sauce
4. Return to the air fryer and cook for 5 minutes

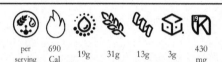
# 4.14 Onion Arancini

- Half a packet of risotto
- 3.5 oz breadcrumbs
- 1 tsp onion powder
- 1.2 cups of marinara sauce, pre-warmed
- Salt and pepper

1. Form a rice ball with the risotto
2. Mix the breadcrumbs, onion powder, salt, and pepper
3. Coat the risotto ball in the crumb mix
4. Place in the air fryer, spray with oil, and cook at 390°F for 10 minutes
5. Serve with warm marinara sauce

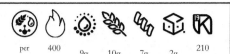
# 4.15 Sweet Potato Wraps

- 1 sweet potato, cubed
- 3 tbsp water
- 10 corn tortillas
- 14 oz black beans
- 1 tsp olive oil
- 1 onion, chopped
- 1 tsp garlic, minced
- 1 chipotle pepper, chopped
- 0.5 tsp cumin
- 0.5 tsp paprika
- 0.5 chilli powder
- Salt and pepper

1. Place the sweet potato in the air fryer spray and cook for 12 minutes at 390°F

2. Heat oil in a pan, add the onion and garlic, and cook for a few minutes until soft

3. Add remaining ingredients to the pan, add 2 tbsp of water and combine

4. Add the sweet potato and 1 tbsp of water and mix

5. Warm the tortilla in the microwave for about 1 minute

6. Place a row of filling across the centre of each tortilla. Fold up the the tortilla

7. Place in the air fryer and cook for about 12 minutes

# CHAPTER 5
# SIDE DISH RECIPES

## 5.1 Crunchy Ranch Potatoes

| per serving | 390 Cal | 4g | 8g | 4g | 1g | 300 mg |

- 1 tbsp olive oil
- 10 oz baby potatoes, cut in half
- 3 tbsp dry ranch seasoning

1. Take a mixing bowl and combine the olive oil with the ranch seasoning
2. Add the potatoes to the bowl and toss to coat
3. Cook for 15 minutes at 395°F, shaking halfway through

## 5.2 Cheesy Carrot Chips

| per serving | 300 Cal | 9g | 10g | 7g | 1g | 320 mg |

- 1 tbsp olive oil
- 6 oz carrots, halved
- 1 garlic clove, crushed
- 2 tbsp grated parmesan
- Salt and pepper for seasoning

1. Combine the olive oil and garlic
2. Add the carrots to the bowl and toss well
3. Add the parmesan and coat the carrots well
4. Add to the air fryer and cook for 20 minutes at 390°F, shaking at the halfway point

## 5.3 Spicy Rice

per serving | 400 Cal | 3g | 9g | 6g | 1g | 50 mg

- 3 tbsp olive oil
- 17 oz long grain rice, washed
- 1 onion, chopped
- 2 cups of chicken stock
- 0.25 cups of water
- 1 tsp chilli powder
- 0.25 tsp cumin
- 2 tbsp tomato paste
- 0.5 tsp garlic powder
- 1 tsp red pepper flakes
- Half a small jalapeño pepper with seeds out, chopped
- Salt and pepper

1. Add the water and tomato paste and combine, placing to one side
2. Take a baking pan and add a little oil
3. Place the rice on the baking pan
4. Add the chicken stock, tomato paste, jalapeños, onions, and the rest of the olive oil, and combine
5. Place tin foil over the top and place it in your air fryer
6. Cook at 390°F for 50 minutes

## 5.4 Garlic Asparagus

per serving | 200 Cal | 9g | 10g | 7g | 1g | 210 mg

- 1 tsp olive oil
- 17 oz asparagus
- 1 tsp garlic salt
- 1 tbsp parmesan cheese, grated
- Salt and pepper

1. Place the asparagus in the air fryer with the oil
2. Sprinkle the parmesan and garlic salt on top, and season
3. Cook for between 7 and 10 minutes at 360°F

## 5.5 Tasty Potato Wedges

per serving | 210 Cal | 9g | 15g | 4g | 1g | 220 mg

- 2 potatoes, cut into wedges
- 1.5 tbsp olive oil
- 0.5 tsp chilli powder
- 0.5 tsp paprika
- Salt and pepper

1. Add all ingredients to a bowl and combine well
2. Place the wedges into the air fryer and cook for 10 minutes at 390°F
3. Turn and cook for a further 8 minutes

---

## 5.6 Avocado Chips

per serving | 380 Cal | 5g | 4g | 7g | 1g | 390 mg

- 1 egg
- 1 sliced avocado
- 3.5 oz breadcrumbs
- 5 oz flour
- 1 tsp water
- Salt and pepper

1. Mix flour salt and pepper together in a bowl
2. Beat egg and water together in another bowl and add bread crumbs to a third
3. Dip the avocado into the flour, then the egg then into the breadcrumbs
4. Spray with cooking oil and place in the air fryer
5. Cook for 4 minutes at 390°F, turn then cook for a further 3 minutes

# 5.7 Fruity Tofu

| per serving | 190 Cal | 2g | 7g | 3g | 1g | 400 mg |

- 14 oz tofu, drained and cut into cubes
- 1 tbsp maple syrup
- 0.3 cups of orange juice
- 2 tsp cornstarch
- 1 tbsp tamari
- 1 tbsp corn starch
- 0.25 tsp pepper flakes
- 0.3 cups of orange juice
- 1 tsp orange zest
- 1 tsp ginger, minced
- 1 tsp fresh garlic
- 0.3 cups of water

1. Place the tofu in a bowl add the tamari, combine
2. Mix in 1 tbsp starch and allow to sit for 30 minutes
3. Place the remaining ingredients into another bowl and mix well
4. Place the tofu in the air fryer and cook at 370°F for about 10 minutes
5. Add tofu to a pan with the sauce mixture and cook until the sauce thickens

# 5.8 Parsley Courgette

| per serving | 290 Cal | 9g | 4g | 3g | 1g | 250 mg |

- 2 courgettes, cut in half lengthways and sliced
- 1 tbsp vegetable oil
- 1 tbsp chopped parsley
- 2 tbsp breadcrumbs
- 4 tbsp grated parmesan
- Salt and pepper

1. Heat the air fryer to 360°F
2. Mix all ingredients together except for the courgette
3. Place the courgette in the air fryer and top with the breadcrumbs
4. Cook for about 15 minutes at 370°F

# 5.9 Stuffed Pumpkin

| per serving | 180 Cal | 7g | 9g | 6g | 1g | 800 mg |

- 1/2 pumpkin, seeds removed
- 1 egg
- 1 sweet potato, chopped
- 1 parsnip, chopped
- 1 onion, chopped
- 1 carrot, chopped
- 2 tsp dried mixed herbs
- 1 oz peas
- 2 garlic cloves, minced

1. Combine all ingredients in a bowl, except for the pumpkin
2. Stuff the pumpkin with the mixture
3. Place the pumpkin in the air fryer and cook for about 30 minutes at 370°F

# 5.10 Marinated Cauliflower

| per serving | 190 Cal | 4g | 9g | 5g | 2g | 300 mg |

- 0.4 cups of water
- 1 small cauliflower, divided into florets
- 1 onion, sliced
- 1 oz cornstarch
- 1.7 oz flour
- 2 tbsp tomato ketchup
- 2 tbsp brown sugar
- Salt and pepper

1. Mix together flour, cornstarch, water, salt, and pepper until smooth
2. Coat the cauliflower and chill for 30 minutes
3. Place in the air fryer and cook for 22 minutes at 370°F
4. Meanwhile combine remaining ingredients in a saucepan, gently simmer until thickened.
5. Serve the cauliflower with the sauce on top

# CHAPTER 6
# POULTRY RECIPES

## 6.1 Turkey in Mushroom Sauce

| | | | | | |
|---|---|---|---|---|---|
| per serving | 426 Cal | 21g | 18g | 5g | 1g | 260 mg |

- 1 can of mushroom soup
- 0.6 cups of milk
- 2 turkey cutlets
- 1 tbsp butter
- Salt and pepper

1. Brush the turkey cutlets with the butter and seasoning
2. Place in the air fryer and cook for 11 minutes at 390°F
3. Add the mushroom soup and milk to a pan and cook over the stove for around 10 minutes, stirring every so often
4. Pour the sauce over the cutlets

## 6.2 Zingy Lemon Chicken Wings

| | | | | | |
|---|---|---|---|---|---|
| per serving | 356 Cal | 6g | 31g | 7g | 3g | 120 mg |

- 2.2lb chicken wings
- 1/4 tsp cayenne pepper
- 2 tsp lemon pepper seasoning, plus an extra 1tsp for the sauce
- 3 tbsp butter
- 1 tsp honey

1. Preheat the air fryer to 260C
2. Place the lemon pepper seasoning and cayenne in a bowl and combine
3. Coat the chicken in the seasoning
4. Place the chicken in the air fryer and cook for 20 minutes, turning over halfway
5. Turn the temperature up to 390°F and cook for another 6 minutes
6. Meanwhile, melt the butter and combine with the honey and the rest of the seasoning
7. Remove the wings from the air fryer and pour the sauce over the top

2 | 5" | 20"

# 6.3 Air Fryer Potatoes With Chicken

| per serving | 390 Cal | 16g | 21g | 7g | 1g | 350 mg |

- 2 tbsp olive oil
- 2 potatoes, cut into 2" pieces
- 2 chicken breast, cut into chunks
- 4 crushed garlic cloves
- 2 tsp smoked paprika
- 1 tsp thyme
- 0.5 tsp red chilli flakes
- Salt and pepper

1. Combine the potatoes with half of the garlic, half the paprika, half the chilli flakes, salt, pepper, and half the oil

2. Place into the air fryer and cook for 5 minutes at 360°F, before turning over and cooking for another 5 minutes

3. Take a bowl and add the chicken with the rest of the seasonings and oil, until totally coated

4. Add the chicken to the potatoes mixture, moving the potatoes to the side

5. Cook for 10 minutes, turning the chicken halfway through

---

2 | 5" | 15"

# 6.4 Spicy Tandoori Chicken

| per serving | 500 Cal | 4g | 19g | 8g | 2g | 210 mg |

- 17 oz chicken tenders, cut into halves
- 1 tbsp minced ginger
- 1 tbsp minced garlic
- 1 tsp cayenne pepper
- 1 tsp turmeric
- 1 tsp garam masala
- 0.3 cups of yogurt
- 0.8 oz coriander leaves
- Salt and pepper

1. Combine all the ingredients, except the chicken

2. Once combined, add the chicken to the bowl and make sure it is fully coated

3. Preheat the air fryer to 370°F and cook the chicken for 10 minutes

4. Turn over and cook for another 5 minutes

**6.5 Turkey and Mushroom Burgers**

2 | 5" | 10"

per serving | 360 Cal | 10g | 19g | 5g | 2g | 290 mg

- 6 oz mushrooms
- 17 oz minced turkey
- 1 tbsp of chicken seasoning
- 1 tsp onion powder
- 1 tsp garlic powder
- Salt and pepper

1. Puree the mushrooms in a food processor
2. Add all the seasonings and mix well
3. Transfer the mixture to a mixing bowl
4. Add the minced turkey and combine again
5. Shape the mix into 5 patties
6. Spray with cooking spray and place in the air fryer
7. Cook at 360°F for 10 minutes, until cooked

---

**6.6 Smoked Chicken**

1 | 5" | 20"

per serving | 432 Cal | 4g | 9g | 5g | 2g | 210 mg

- 2 chicken breasts, halved
- 2 tsp olive oil
- 1 tsp ground thyme
- 2 tsp paprika
- 1tsp cumin
- 0.5 tsp cayenne pepper
- 0.5 tsp onion powder
- Salt and pepper

1. Combine the spices together
2. Pour the spice mixture onto a plate
3. Take each chicken breast and coat in the spices, pressing down to ensure an even distribution
4. Place the chicken to one side for 5 minutes
5. Preheat your air fryer to 370°F
6. Arrange the chicken inside the fryer and cook for 10 minutes
7. Turn the chicken over and cook for another 10 minutes
8. Remove from the fryer and allow to sit for 5 minutes before serving

## 6.7 Chicken Thighs in Bacon

| per serving | 390 Cal | 12g | 18g | 9g | 1g | 300 mg |

- 2.6 oz butter, softened
- 3.5 oz bacon
- 12 oz boneless chicken thighs
- 0.5 clove garlic, minced
- 0.25 tsp dried thyme
- 0.25 tsp dried basil
- Salt and pepper

1. Combine the softened butter, garlic, thyme, basil, salt, and pepper
2. Place the butter onto a sheet of plastic wrap and roll it up to make a butter log
3. Refrigerate for at least 1 hour and remove the plastic wrap
4. Place one bacon strip onto the butter and then place the chicken thighs on top of the bacon
5. Place the cold butter into the middle of the chicken thigh and tuck one end of bacon into the chicken
6. Next, fold over the chicken thigh whilst rolling the bacon around
7. Cook the chicken until white in the centre and the juices run clear, at 370°F

---

## 6.8 Chicken With a Bang!

| per serving | 450 Cal | 17g | 22g | 9g | 2g | 290 mg |

- 17 oz chicken breasts, cut into pieces
- 1 egg, beaten
- 0.2 cups of milk
- 1 tbsp hot pepper sauce
- 2 oz flour
- 2.4 oz tapioca starch
- 1.5 tsp seasoned starch
- 1 tsp garlic granules
- 0.5 tsp cumin
- 6 tbsp plain Greek yogurt
- 3 tbsp sweet chilli sauce
- 1 tsp hot sauce

1. Take a mixing bowl and combine the egg, milk, and hot sauce
2. Take another bowl and combine the flour, tapioca starch, salt, garlic, and cumin
3. Dip the chicken pieces into the sauce bowl and then into the flour bowl
4. Place the chicken into the air fryer at 350°F and cook for 15 minutes
5. Whilst cooking, mix together the Greek yogurt, sweet chilli sauce, and hot sauce and serve with the chicken

## 6.9 Chicken Fried Rice

| per serving | 390 Cal | 7g | 13g | 10g | 1g | 260 mg |

- 14 oz white rice, cooked
- 14 oz cooked chicken, cut into pieces
- 7 oz peas and carrots mix
- 1 onion, diced
- 6 tbsp soy sauce
- 1 tbsp vegetable oil

1. Combine the rice, vegetable oil, and soy sauce
2. Add the peas, carrots, diced onion, and the chicken and mix together well
3. Pour the mixture into a nonstick pan and place in the air fryer
4. Cook at 360°F for 20 minutes

   2 | 1' | 12"

## 6.10 Sticky Chicken Thighs

| per serving | 550 Cal | 13g | 19g | 8g | 2g | 210 mg |

- 4 bone-in chicken thighs
- 0.8 cups of buttermilk
- ½ tbsp maple syrup
- 1 egg
- 1 tsp granulated garlic salt
- 4.9 oz all-purpose flour
- 2.2 oz tapioca flour
- 1 tsp sweet paprika
- 1 tsp onion powder
- 0.25 tsp ground black pepper
- 0.25 tsp cayenne pepper
- 0.5 tsp granulated garlic
- 0.5 tsp honey powder

1. Combine the buttermilk, maple syrup, egg, and garlic powder
2. Transfer to a bag and add chicken thighs, shaking to combine well
3. Set aside for 1 hour
4. Take a shallow bowl and add the flour, tapioca flour, salt, sweet paprika, smoked paprika, pepper, cayenne pepper, and honey powder, combining well
5. Preheat the air fryer to 320°F
6. Drag the chicken through the flour mixture and place the chicken skin side down in the air fryer
7. Cook for 12 minutes, until white in the middle

**6.11 Cayenne Wings**

| per serving | 346 Cal | 5g | 30g | 7g | 2g | 30 mg |
|---|---|---|---|---|---|---|

- 2lb chicken wings
- 1 tsp honey
- 0.25 tsp cayenne pepper
- 2 tsp lemon pepper seasoning
- 3 tbsp melted butter

1. Preheat your air fryer to 550F
2. Take a bowl and mix together the cayenne and lemon pepper
3. Add the chicken and coat everything well
4. Place inside the air fryer and cook for 10 minutes on each side
5. Increase the temperature to 570F and cook for another 6 minutes
6. Mix the honey and melted butter together and pour over the chicken once cooked

---

**6.12 Easy Chicken Nuggets**

| per serving | 213 Cal | 26g | 9g | 26g | 3g | 50 mg |
|---|---|---|---|---|---|---|

- 8 chicken tenders
- 50oz breadcrumbs
- 1 beaten egg
- 2 tbsp olive oil

1. Mix together the oil and breadcrumbs in a large bowl
2. Dip each tender in the egg, and then the breadcrumbs, coating evenly
3. Place inside the air fryer
4. Repeat with all tenders
5. Cook for 12 minutes at 340F

## 6.13 Chicken & Jalapeño Chimichangas

| per serving | 406 Cal | 21g | 26g | 26g | 4g | 55 mg |

- 6 tortillas (flour)
- 3.5oz cooked chicken, shredded
- 1 chopped jalapeño pepper
- 2oz refried beans
- 5oz nacho cheese
- 1 tsp cumin
- 0.5 tsp chilli powder
- 5 tbsp salsa
- Salt and pepper for seasoning

1. Take a large bowl and combine all ingredients, except the tortillas
2. Place a little of the filling into each tortilla and roll up, sealing the edges
3. Place inside the air fryer
4. Cook at 390F for 7 minutes

## 6.14 Paprika & Garlic Chicken

| per serving | 305 Cal | 41g | 26g | 20g | 4g | 55 mg |

- 17oz boneless chicken thighs
- 0.5 tsp brown sugar
- 2.6oz flour
- 1.4 oz tapioca flour
- 1 cup of buttermilk
- 1 beaten egg
- 1 tsp garlic powder
- 0.5 tsp garlic salt
- 0.5 tsp onion powder
- 0.25 tsp oregano
- 0.5 tsp paprika
- Salt and pepper for seasoning

1. Combine the buttermilk, maple syrup, egg, and garlic powder
2. Transfer to a bag and add chicken thighs, shaking to combine well
3. Set aside for 1 hour
4. Take a shallow bowl and add the flour, tapioca flour, salt, sweet paprika, smoked paprika, pepper, cayenne pepper, and honey powder, combining well
5. Preheat the air fryer to 320°F
6. Drag the chicken through the flour mixture and place the chicken skin side down in the air fryer
7. Cook for 12 minutes, until white in the middle

# 6.15 Turkey Bites

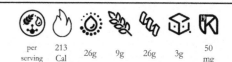

| | | | | | | |
|---|---|---|---|---|---|---|
| per serving | 213 Cal | 26g | 9g | 26g | 3g | 50 mg |

- 17oz ground turkey
- 50oz breadcrumbs
- 1 beaten egg
- 2 tbsp olive oil

1. Mix together the oil and breadcrumbs in a large bowl
2. Take the ground turkey and create small patties with your hands
3. Dip the patties into the breadcrumb mixture
4. Place inside the air fryer
5. Repeat the same process with the remaining turkey mixture
6. Cook for 12 minutes at 340F

# CHAPTER 7
# PORK RECIPES

## 7.1 Pork Tenderloin in Dijon Mustard

2 | 35" | 30"

per serving | 450 Cal | 9g | 14g | 8g | 1g | 390 mg

- 1 pork tenderloin
- 3 tbsp soy sauce
- 2 minced garlic cloves
- 3 tbsp olive oil
- 2 tbsp brown sugar
- 1 tbsp dijon mustard
- Salt and pepper

1. Take a bowl and combine the ingredients, except for the pork
2. Pour the mixture into a ziplock bag and then add the pork
3. Close the top and make sure the pork is well covered
4. Place in the refrigerator for 30 minutes
5. Preheat your air fryer to 380°F
6. Remove the pork from the bag and place it in the fryer
7. Cook for 25 minutes, turning halfway
8. Remove and rest for 5 minutes before slicing into pieces

## 7.2 Breaded Pork Chops

2 | 5" | 10"

per serving | 300 Cal | 9g | 5g | 6g | 1g | 300 mg

- Dressings:
- Salt and pepper
- 0.5 tsp paprika,
- 0.5 tsp thyme,
- 0.5 tsp onion powder
- 0.5 tsp garlic powder
- 2 tbsp mayonnaise
- 2 pork chops
- 8 oz Italian breadcrumbs

1. Combine the breadcrumbs, garlic powder, paprika, salt and pepper, and thyme, and onion powder
2. Cover the pork chops with the mayonnaise making sure to cover both sides
3. Coat the meat with the seasoning mixture, making sure it is fully covered
4. Cook the pork chops in the fryer for 10 minutes at 380°F, turning over halfway

## 7.3 Pork & Marinara Sub

per serving | 390 Cal | 6g | 12g | 6g | 1g | 290 mg

- 8 pork meatballs
- 5 tbsp marinara sauce
- 5 oz grated cheese
- 2 hotdog rolls
- 0.25 tsp dried oregano

1. Place the meatballs in the air fryer and cook for around 10 minutes, turning halfway through
2. Coat the meatballs in the marinara sauce
3. Cover with the oregano
4. Take the bread roll and add the mixture inside
5. Top with the cheese
6. Place the meatball sub back in the air fryer and cook for 2 minutes at 390°F

## 7.4 BBQ Ribs

per serving | 554 Cal | 21g | 19g | 10g | 1g | 300 mg

- Dressings: 0.5 tsp five spice
- 1 tsp sesame oil,
- 1 tsp salt,
- 1 tsp black pepper,
- 1 tsp soy sauce
- 3 chopped garlic cloves
- 4 tbsp bbq sauce
- 1 tbsp honey
- 17 oz ribs

1. Chop the ribs into small pieces and place them in a bowl
2. Add all the ingredients into the bowl and mix well
3. Marinate for 4 hours
4. Preheat the air fryer to 350°F
5. Place the ribs into the air fryer and cook for 14 minutes
6. Coat the ribs in honey and cook for a further 16 minutes

# 7.5 Pork Schnitzel

| | | | | | |
|---|---|---|---|---|---|
| per serving | 426 Cal | 21g | 22g | 14g | 2g | 320 mg |

- 3 pork steaks, cut into cubes
- 2 eggs
- 6 oz flour
- 6 oz breadcrumbs
- Salt and pepper

1. Season the pork with salt and pepper
2. Coat the pork in the flour and then dip in the egg
3. Coat the pork in breadcrumbs
4. Place in the air fryer and cook at 350°F for 20 minutes, turning halfway

# 7.6 Fruity Balsamic Pork Chops

| | | | | | |
|---|---|---|---|---|---|
| per serving | 579 Cal | 30g | 20g | 10g | 1g | 310 mg |

- 4 pork chops
- 2 eggs
- 0.1 cups of milk
- 8 oz breadcrumbs
- 8 oz pecans, finely chopped
- 1 tbsp orange juice
- 0.1 cups of balsamic vinegar
- 2 tbsp brown sugar
- 2 tbsp raspberry jam

1. Mix the eggs and milk together in a bowl
2. In another bowl mix the breadcrumbs and pecans
3. Coat the pork chops in flour, egg and then coat in the breadcrumbs
4. Place in the air fryer and cook for 12 minutes at 390°F, turning halfway
5. Put the remaining ingredients in a pan simmer for about 6 minutes
6. Serve the sauce with the pork chops

# 7.7 Chinese Spiced Pork

| per serving | 510 Cal | 32g | 19g | 15g | 2g | 330 mg |

- 2 pork rounds, cut into chunks
- 2 eggs
- 1 tsp sesame oil
- 7 oz cornstarch
- 0.25 tsp salt
- 0.5 tsp pepper
- 3 tbsp canola oil
- 1 tsp Chinese five spice

1. Mix the corn starch, salt, pepper, and five spice together
2. Mix the eggs and sesame oil in another bowl
3. Dip the pork into the egg and then cover in the cornstarch mix
4. Place in the air fryer and cook at 340°F for 11-12 minutes, shaking halfway through

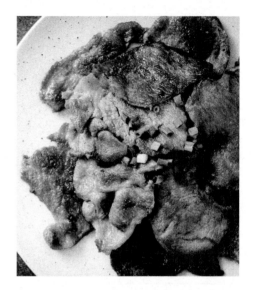

---

# 7.8 Pineapple Pork

| per serving | 256 Cal | 10g | 15g | 7g | 2g | 300 mg |

- Dressings:
- 1 tbsp oil,
- 2 tbsp soy,
- 1 tbsp brown sugar,
- 0.5 tsp pepper,
- 0.5 tsp salt
- 1 tsp ginger
- 1 clove of garlic, minced
- 1 red pepper, sliced
- 2.6 oz fresh coriander, chopped
- Half a pineapple, cut into cubes
- 15 oz pork loin, cubed

1. Add salt and pepper to the pork
2. Place all ingredients in the air fryer and cook for 17 minutes at 350°F.
3. Serve with coriander garnish

4 | 5" | 15"

# 7.9 Seasoned Belly Pork

| per serving | 332 Cal | 24g | 10g | 10g | 2g | 350 mg |

- 17 oz belly pork
- Salt and pepper

1. Cut the pork into bite-size pieces and season with salt and pepper
2. Heat the air fryer to 390°F
3. Cook for 15 minutes, until crisp

---

   4 | 5" | 10"

# 7.10 Pork & Ginger Meatballs

| per serving | 386 Cal | 20g | 21g | 10g | 1g | 210 mg |

 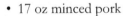

- 17 oz minced pork
- 2 eggs
- 3.5 oz breadcrumbs
- 2 spring onions, diced
- 1 tsp minced garlic
- 0.5 tsp chilli flakes
- 1 tsp minced ginger
- 1 tsp sesame oil
- 1 tsp soy sauce
- Salt and pepper

1. Mix all ingredients in a bowl
2. Form mix into 1.5" sized meatballs
3. Place in the air fryer and cook at 390°F for about 10 minutes
4.

# CHAPTER 8
# BEEF RECIPES

---

2 | 1' | 5"

## 8.1 Steak & Asparagus Cubes

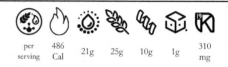
per serving | 486 Cal | 21g | 25g | 10g | 1g | 310 mg

- 17 oz steak, cut into cubes
- 0.3 cups of Tamari sauce
- 2 garlic cloves, crushed
- 8 oz asparagus, trimmed
- 3 large bell peppers, sliced
- 2 tbsp butter
- Salt and pepper

1. Season the steak to your liking
2. Place the meat in a zip-top bag and add the Tamari and garlic, sealing the bag closed. Leave in the refrigerator for at least 1 hour
3. Remove the steaks from the bag and throw the marinade away
4. Place the peppers and sliced asparagus in the centre of each steak piece
5. Roll the steak up and secure it in place
6. Transfer the meat parcels to the air fryer and cook for 5 minutes at 390°F
7. Melt the butter in a saucepan, adding the juices from the air fryer, cooking until thickened
8. Pour the sauce over the steak

---

2 | 5" | 9"

## 8.2 Mexican Steak & Chips

per serving | 436 Cal | 22g | 22g | 9g | 1g | 360 mg

- 17 oz sirloin steak
- 1 bag of French fries
- 12 oz grated cheese
- 2 tbsp sour cream
- 2 tbsp guacamole
- 2 tbsp steak seasoning
- Salt and pepper

1. Place in the air fryer and cook for 4 minutes at 360°F
2. Turn over and cooking for another 4 minutes
3. Remove and allow to rest
4. Add the French fries to the fryer and cook for 5 minutes, shaking regularly
5. Add the cheese
6. Cut the steak into pieces and add on top of the cheese
7. Cook for another 30 seconds, until the cheese is melted

5 | 1' | 35"

# 8.3 Beef Wellington

| per serving | 256 Cal | 9g | 10g | 6g | 2g | 380 mg |

- 17 oz shortcrust pastry
- 21 oz beef fillet
- 10 oz chicken pate
- 1 egg, beaten
- Salt and pepper

1. Season the beef and wrap in plastic wrap. Place in the refrigerator for 1 hour
2. Roll out the pastry and brush the egg over the edges
3. Spread the pate over the pastry
4. Remove the clingfilm from the beef and place it in the centre of the pastry, sealing around the meat
5. Place in the air fryer and cook at 330°F for 35 minutes

---

2 | 5" | 25"

# 8.4 Coconut Asian Beef

| per serving | 356 Cal | 33g | 15g | 10g | 1g | 400 mg |

- 1 tbsp coconut oil
- 21 oz steak, cut into slices
- 2 red peppers, sliced
- 0.4 cups of liquid aminos
- 0.4 cups of water
- 3.5 oz brown sugar
- 0.5 tsp ground ginger
- 0.5 tbsp minced garlic
- 1 tsp red pepper flakes
- Salt and pepper

1. In a pan, melt the coconut oil and sauté the peppers until tender.
2. In another pan add the pepper flakes, garlic, ginger, brown sugar and aminos. Mix and bring to the boil, simmering for 10 mins
3. Place the steak in the air fryer for 10 minutes at 360°F
4. Turn over and cook for a further 5 minutes
5. Combine the beef with the peppers and sauce

# 8.5 Beef Fried Rice

| per serving | 325 Cal | 46g | 14g | 7g | 1g | 330 mg |

- 14 oz rice, cooked
- 1 tbsp vegetable oil
- 8 oz beef strips, pre-cooked
- 8 oz peas
- 1 tbsp sesame oil
- 1 onion, diced
- 1 egg
- 2 tsp garlic powder
- Salt and pepper

1. Season the beef with salt, pepper, and garlic powder, cook in a pan until about ¾ done
2. Mix the rice with peas carrots and vegetable oil, add the beef, and mix
3. Add to the air fryer and cook for about 10 minutes at 370°F
4. Add the egg and cook

# 8.6 Feta Hamburgers

| per serving | 334 Cal | 22g | 10g | 9g | 1g | 310 mg |

- 14 oz minced beef
- 8 oz feta, crumbled
- 0.8 oz green olives, chopped
- 0.5 tsp garlic powder
- 0.5 cup onion, chopped
- 2 tbsp Worcestershire sauce
- 0.5 tsp steak seasoning
- Salt and pepper

1. Mix all the ingredients in a bowl
2. Divide the mix into four and shape into patties
3. Place in the air fryer and cook at 390°F for about 15 minutes

## 8.7 Stuffed Peppers With Beef

- 17 oz minced beef
- 4 bell peppers, tops and seeds removed
- 2.5 oz rice, cooked
- Half a chopped onion
- 1 garlic clove, minced
- 5 tbsp tomato sauce
- 3.5 oz grated cheese
- 2 tsp Worcestershire sauce
- 1 tsp garlic powder
- 0.5 tsp chilli powder
- 1 tsp dried basil
- Salt and pepper

1. Cook the onions, minced beef, garlic, and all the seasonings until the meat is browned
2. Remove from the heat and add Worcestershire sauce, rice, half the cheese, and most of the tomato sauce. Mix well
3. Stuff the peppers with the mixture and place in the air fryer
4. Cook at 390°F for 11 minutes
5. Toward the end of the cooking time, add the rest of the tomato sauce and cheese

## 8.8 Paprika Steak And Mushrooms

- Dressings:
- 1 tsp paprika,
- 1 tsp parsley flakes,
- 1 tbsp olive oil,
- 3 tbsp Worcestershire sauce
- 10 oz button mushrooms
- 17 oz sirloin steak, cut into cubes
- 1 tsp crushed chilli flakes

1. Combine all Ingredients in a bowl, cover, and chill for at least 4 hours
2. Place the steak and mushrooms in the air fryer and cook for 5 minutes at 390°F
3. Shake and cook for a further 5 minutes

## 8.9 Beef Enchiladas

| per serving | 546 Cal | 20g | 26g | 5g | 2g | 390 mg |

- 17 oz minced beef
- 8 flour tortillas
- 1 packet taco seasoning
- 10 oz grated cheese
- 5 oz sour cream
- 1 can of black beans
- 1 can chopped tomatoes
- 1 can mild chopped chillies
- 1 can red enchilada sauce
- 10 oz coriander, chopped

1. Brown the beef and add the taco seasoning
2. Add the beef, beans, tomatoes, and chillies to the tortillas
3. Line the air fryer with foil and put the tortillas in
4. Pour the enchilada sauce over the top and sprinkle with cheese
5. Cook at 390°F for five minutes

---

## 8.10 Spicy Steak Wraps

| per serving | 220 Cal | 10g | 9g | 5g | 1g | 350 mg |

- 17 oz steak, sliced
- 0.8 oz pineapple juice
- 1 onion, sliced
- 1 pepper, sliced
- 2 tbsp lime juice
- 1 tbsp olive oil
- 1 tbsp soy sauce
- 1 tbsp minced garlic
- 0.5 tbsp chilli powder
- 1/2 tsp paprika
- 1 tsp cumin
- Salt and pepper

1. Mix the pineapple juice, lime juice, olive oil, soy sauce, garlic, cumin chilli powder, and paprika. Pour over the steak and marinate for 4 hours
2. Add the peppers and onions inside the air fryer, season with salt and pepper
3. Cook at 200°C for 10 minutes, add the steak and cook for another 7 minutes
4. Place the mixture inside the tortillas and place inside the air fryer
5. Cook for 4 minutes at 350°F
6. Turn over and cook for another 3 minutes

# CHAPTER 9
# LAMB RECIPES

**2** | **15"** | **18"**

## 9.1 Classic Lamb Patties

| per serving | 478 Cal | 19g | 20g | 10g | 2g | 300 mg |

- 21 oz minced lamb
- 2 tsp garlic puree
- 1 tsp harissa paste
- Salt and pepper

1. Place all the ingredients in a bowl and mix well
2. Form into patties
3. Place in the air fryer and cook at 340°F for 18 minutes

---

**2** | **5"** | **11"**

## 9.2 Lamb & Worcestershire Sauce Peppers

| per serving | 332 Cal | 10g | 12g | 10g | 2g | 350 mg |

- 4 bell peppers, tops and seeds removed
- 17 oz minced lamb
- 2.6 oz rice, cooked
- Half an onion, chopped
- 1 garlic clove, minced
- 5 tbsp tomato sauce
- 2 tsp Worcestershire sauce
- 3.5 oz grated cheese
- 1 tsp garlic powder
- 0.5 tsp chilli powder
- 1 tsp dried basil
- Salt and pepper

1. Cook the onions, minced lamb, garlic, and seasonings until the meat is browned
2. Remove from the heat and add Worcestershire sauce, rice, cheese, and tomato sauce
3. Place the mixture inside the peppers and place in the air fryer
4. Cook at 390°F for about 11 minutes

# 9.3 Lamb & Jalapeño Empanadas

| | per serving | 300 Cal | 10g | 16g | 10g | 1g | 390 mg |

- 2 tsp olive oil
- 2 packs of shortcrust pastry
- 17 oz minced lamb
- 1 egg, beaten
- 1 onion, chopped
- 1 clove garlic, chopped
- 2 tbsp jalapeño, chopped
- 3.5 oz cheddar cheese, grated
- Salt and pepper

1. Heat the oil in a pan and fry the onion and garlic until soft
2. Add the meat and jalapeño, season with salt and pepper, and cook until browned
3. Allow the meat to cool
4. Roll out dough as thin as possible and cut into circles
5. Add some of the mixture and top with cheese
6. Fold over the edges and brush with the beaten egg
7. Cook for about 12 minutes at 350°F

# 9.4 Lamb Kebabs

| | per serving | 290 Cal | 4g | 9g | 5g | 2g | 310 mg |

- 17 oz lamb, cubed
- 0.8 oz sour cream
- 1 bell pepper, cut into chunks
- Half an onion, cut into chunks
- 2 tbsp soy sauce
- 8 metal skewers

1. Mix the sour cream and soy sauce in a bowl
2. Add the lamb and marinate for at least 30 minutes
3. Thread beef, bell peppers, and onion onto skewers
4. Cook in the air fryer at 390°F for 10 minutes, turning halfway

## 9.5 Lamb & Ginger Burgers

- Dressings:
- 1 tbsp olive oil
- 2 tsp sugar
- 1 tbsp soy
- 2 tsp ginger, minced
- 2 tsp garlic, minced
- 1 onion, chopped
- 17 oz minced lamb

1. Combine all ingredients and rest for at least 30 minutes in the refrigerator
2. Divide the meat into four and form into patties
3. Place in the air fryer and cook at 370°F for 10 minutes

## 9.6 Cheesy Lamb Balls

- 2 tbsp taco seasoning
- 1 tbsp water
- 17 oz ground lamb
- 1 can of green chillis, chopped
- 1 egg white, beaten
- 16 small cubes of cheddar cheese
- 10 oz tortilla chips, crushed

1. Combine the lamb with the green chillies and taco seasoning
2. Create small meatballs out of the mixture
3. Place a cube of cheese in the middle of each meatball and close around the edges
4. Dip every meatball into the egg white and then the crushed chips
5. Place the balls into the air fryer and cook at 370°F for 14 minutes, turning halfway

# 9.7 Spicy Lamb Meatloaf

- Dressings:
- Salt and pepper
- 0.5 tsp cinnamon
- 1 tsp turmeric
- 1 tsp cayenne
- 2 tsp garam masala
- 1 tbsp minced garlic
- ⅛ cardamom pod
- 1 tbsp ginger, minced
- 7 oz coriander, sliced
- 1 onion, diced
- 2 eggs
- 17 oz minced lamb

1. Place all the Ingredients in a large bowl and combine
2. Form a loaf shape with the mixture and place in the air fryer
3. Cook for 15 minutes at 360°F
4. Slice before serving

# 9.8 Mushroom & Onion "Pasties"

- 10 oz minced lamb
- 1 tbsp olive oil
- 1 egg, beaten
- 8 gyoza wrappers
- 1 onion, chopped
- 5 oz mushrooms, chopped
- 4 tomatoes, chopped
- 6 green olives
- 0.5 tsp cinnamon
- 2 tsp garlic, chopped
- 0.25 tsp paprika
- 0.25 tsp cumin

1. Heat the oil in a pan. Add the onion and minced lamb. Cook until browned
2. Add the mushrooms and cook for 6 minutes more
3. Add garlic, olives, paprika, cumin, and cinnamon, and cook for about 3 minutes
4. Stir in tomatoes and cook for 1 minute. Place the mixture to one side for 20 minutes
5. Place a spoonful of the mixture into each wrapper
6. Brush the edges with egg and fold over to seal
7. Place in the air fryer and cook at 390°F for 7 minutes

# 9.9 Lasagne Taco Bake

per serving | 390 Cal | 20g | 25g | 10g | 2g | 370 mg

- 15 oz ground lamb
- 2 tbsp olive oil
- 2 flour tortillas
- 1 onion, chopped
- 1 garlic clove, minced
- 8 oz grated cheese
- 3.8 oz tomato sauce
- 1 tsp cumin
- 1 tsp oregano

1. Cook the onions with the oil in a frying pan, until soft
2. Add the lamb and garlic and cook until the meat has browned
3. Add the tomato sauce, cumin, and oregano and cook for 2 minutes
4. Place one tortilla on the bottom of your air fryer basket
5. Add a meat layer, followed by cheese, and continue until you have no ingredients left
6. Top with the remaining tortillas
7. Cook at 370ºF for 8 minutes

# 9.10 Lamb & Parsley Roll

per serving | 440 Cal | 20g | 21g | 9g | 1g | 360 mg

- 2 tbsp olive oil
- 14 oz lamb
- 1 onion, sliced
- 4 tbsp dijon mustard
- 4 sliced of bacon, chopped
- 4 tbsp sour cream
- 1 tbsp tomato paste
- 1 tsp parsley, chopped

1. Season the onions and cook in the air fryer at 390ºF for 5 minutes
2. Put half the onions in a bowl and mix with sour cream, 2 tsp parsley, and tomato paste
3. Spread the mustard onto the lamb, followed by the onions and the bacon pieces
4. Roll the lamb up and cook in the air fryer for 10 minutes

# CHAPTER 10
# DESSERT RECIPES

  **10.1 Vanilla Biscuits**

| per serving | 226 Cal | 10g | 15g | 2g | 2g | 120 mg |

- 7 oz flour
- 3.5 oz sugar
- 3.5 oz butter
- 1 egg, beaten
- 1 tsp vanilla essence

1. Rub together the flour, butter, and sugar
2. Add the egg and vanilla to form a dough
3. Split the dough into 6 and form it into balls
4. Place in the air fryer cook at 370°F for 15 minutes

   **10.2 Orange Cocoa Dip**

| per serving | 400 Cal | 19g | 17g | 4g | 2g | 170 mg |

- 2 tbsp flour
- 2 eggs
- 4 tbsp caster sugar
- 4 oz dark chocolate
- 4 oz orange juice
- 4 greased ramekin dishes

1. Place the chocolate and butter in a glass dish and melt over a pan of hot water, stir until combined
2. Beat the eggs and sugar together until pale and fluffy
3. Add the orange juice and egg mix to the chocolate and combine
4. Stir in the flour until fully mixed together
5. Transfer the mixture into your ramekins
6. Place in the air fryer and cook at 360°F for 12 minutes
7. Cool before consumption

## 10.3 Delicious Profiteroles

4 | 5" | 10"

per serving | 390 Cal | 27g | 21g | 5g | 2g | 200 mg

- 3.5 oz butter
- 2 tsp icing sugar
- 7 oz plain flour
- 1.7 oz butter
- 6 eggs
- 1.2 cups of water
- 2 tsp vanilla extract
- 1.2 cups of whipped cream
- 3.5 oz milk chocolate
- 2 tbsp whipped cream

1. Place the butter and water in a pan over a medium heat and bring to the boil
2. Remove from the heat and stir in the flour to create a dough
3. Mix in the eggs and stir until mixture is smooth
4. Create the shapes of profiteroles with all the dough and place in the air fryer
5. Cook at 370°F for 10 minutes
6. Meanwhile, combine the whipped cream, vanilla extract, and the icing sugar
7. Separately, melt the butter, and chocolate
8. Pipe the filling into the profiteroles and top with the chocolate

## 10.4 Cherry Parcels

6 | 5" | 10"

per serving | 290 Cal | 4g | 9g | 5g | 2g | 200 mg

- 10 oz shortcrust pastry, cut into six cookie shapes
- 2.6 oz cherry pie filling
- 0.5 tsp milk
- 3 tbsp icing sugar

1. Take your cookie pieces and add an equal amount of cherry filling in the middle of each
2. Fold over and use a fork to seal the edges
3. Cook in the air fryer at 360°F for 10 minutes
4. Mix together the icing sugar and milk
5. Drizzle the mixture over the parcels once cooled

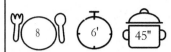

# 10.5 Classic Creamy Cheesecake

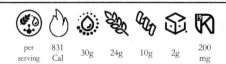

| | | | | | | |
|---|---|---|---|---|---|---|
| per serving | 831 Cal | 30g | 24g | 10g | 2g | 200 mg |

- 7 oz flour
- 0.2 cups of quark
- 3 eggs
- 26 oz cream cheese
- 7 oz sugar
- 3.5 oz brown sugar
- 3.5 oz butter
- 1.7 oz melted butter
- 1 tbsp vanilla essence
- 1 greased springform tin

1. Combine the flour, sugar, and 100g butter
2. Create rough biscuits and place in the air fryer. Cook for 15 minutes at 370°F
3. Once cooked, use a rolling pin to break the biscuits and combine with the melted butter
4. Press the mixture into the bottom of the tin
5. Combine the cream cheese and sugar, add the eggs and vanilla and combine until smooth. Mix in the quark
6. Pour the cheesecake batter into the pan
7. Cook for 30 minutes at 360°F and allow to cool for half an hour
8. Refrigerate for 6 hours

# 10.6 Classic Apple Pie

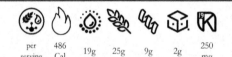

| | | | | | | |
|---|---|---|---|---|---|---|
| per serving | 486 Cal | 19g | 25g | 9g | 2g | 250 mg |

- 1 packet of ready-made pastry
- 1 apple, chopped
- 2 tsp lemon juice
- 1 egg, beaten
- 1 tbsp sugar
- 1 tsp cinnamon
- 2 tbsp sugar
- 0.5 tsp vanilla extract
- 1 tbsp butter

1. Line a baking tin with pastry
2. Mix the apple, lemon juice, cinnamon, sugar, and vanilla in a bowl
3. Pour the apple mix into the tin with the pastry, top with chunks of butter
4. Cover with a second piece of pastry. Pierce slits in the top
5. Brush the pastry with the egg and sprinkle with sugar
6. Place in the air fryer and cook for 30 minutes at 360°F

## 10.7 Chocolate Soufflé

| per serving | 332 Cal | 3g | 24g | 24g | 2g | 134 mg |

- 5 oz milk chocolate, chopped
- 3.5 oz butter
- 2 eggs, separated
- 3 tbsp sugar
- 0.5 tsp vanilla extract
- 2 tbsp flour
- 2 ramekins, greased

1. Melt the chocolate and butter together
2. Separately, beat together the egg yolks, sugar and vanilla
3. Drizzle in the chocolate mix, add the flour, and combine
4. Whisk the egg whites to soft peaks, gently fold into the chocolate mix a little at a time
5. Add the mix to ramekins and place in the air fryer
6. Cook for about 14 minutes at 350°F

## 10.8 Classic Chocolate Cake

| per serving | 573 Cal | 30g | 35g | 5g | 2g | 180 mg |

- 7 oz flour
- 0.8 oz cocoa powder
- 5 oz sugar
- 3 eggs
- 0.3 cups of sour cream
- 2 tsp vanilla extract
- 1 tsp baking powder
- 0.5 tsp baking soda

1. Mix all the ingredients together in a bowl and transfer to a baking tin
2. Place into the air fryer and cook for 25 minutes at 350°

# 10.9 Honey & Apple Pasties

- 1 tsp water
- 2 tsp cornstarch
- 1 tsp nutmeg
- 1 tsp cinnamon
- 1 tsp vanilla extract
- 2 tbsp honey
- 2 apples, diced
- 12 empanada wrappers

1. Combine the apples, cinnamon, honey, vanilla, and nutmeg in a pan and cook for 2-3 minutes
2. Mix the cornstarch and water add to the pan and cook for 30 seconds
3. Add the apple mix to each of the empanada wraps
4. Roll the wrap in half, pinch along the edges, and seal
5. Cook for 8 minutes at 390°F
6. Turn over and cook for another 10 minutes

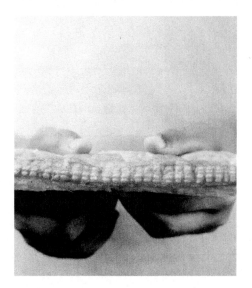

---

# 10.10 Banana & Walnut Bread

- 7 oz flour
- 2 bananas, mashed
- 2 tbsp walnuts, chopped
- 2 eggs
- 2.6 oz sugar
- 1 tsp cinnamon
- 0.5 tsp salt
- 0.25 tsp baking soda
- 0.8 oz plain yogurt
- 2 tbsp oil
- 1 tsp vanilla extract
- 6" cake tin, lined with parchment paper

1. Combine the flour, cinnamon, salt, and baking soda
2. Separately, mix together the remaining ingredients
3. Combine the two mixtures together
4. Transfer into the cake tin and place in the air fryer
5. Cook for 35 minutes at 350°F, turning halfway through

# CHAPTER 11
# SNACK & APPETIZER RECIPES

**11.1 Cheesy Garlic Bread**

| | | | | | | |
|---|---|---|---|---|---|---|
| per serving | 225 Cal | 15g | 19g | 3g | 1g | 210 mg |

- 1 egg
- 10 oz grated cheese
- 0.5 tsp garlic powder

1. Combine the ingredients and create round shapes on a piece of parchment paper
2. Place in the air fryer and cook for 10 minutes at 360°F

---

**11.2 Chicken & Bacon BBQ Bites**

| | | | | | | |
|---|---|---|---|---|---|---|
| per serving | 250 Cal | 4g | 9g | 5g | 2g | 210 mg |

- 2 chicken breasts, cut into strips
- 2 tbsp brown sugar
- 0.8 oz BBQ sauce
- 7 slices of bacon, cut into long pieces

1. Wrap two strips of the bacon around each piece of chicken
2. Brush the tops with the BBQ sauce and add some brown sugar to each
3. Cook for 5 minutes at 390°F, turn and cook for a further 5 minutes

## 11.3 Onion Bhajis

- 1 onion, sliced
- 1 red onion, sliced
- 1 jalapeño pepper, minced
- 5 oz chickpea flour
- 4 tbsp water
- 1 clove garlic, minced
- 1 tsp coriander
- 0.5 tsp cumin
- 1 tsp turmeric
- Salt and pepper

1. Combine all ingredients in a large bowl and create round balls using your hands
2. Cook for 6 minutes on each side at 390°F

## 11.4 Spicy Pork Bites

- 14 oz pork mince
- 2 tsp Thai curry paste
- 1 tbsp Worcester sauce
- Juice and zest of 1 lime
- 1 onion, chopped finely
- 1 tbsp soy sauce
- 1 tsp garlic paste
- 1 tsp coriander
- 1 tsp mixed spice
- Salt and pepper

1. Take a large bowl and combine all ingredients to create a smooth mixture
2. Use your hands to create small balls
3. Refrigerate for half an hour
4. Cook in the air fryer for 15 minutes, at 350°F

# 11.5 Stringy Mozzarella Sticks

| per serving | 686 Cal | 25g | 20g | 8g | 1g | 2180 mg |

- Dressings:
- Salt and pepper,
- 0.5 tsp basil,
- 0.25 tsp oregano,
- 0.5 tsp onion powder,
- 0.5 tsp salt,
- 1 tsp garlic powder
- 0.5 tsp parsley
- 1.7 oz flour
- 1 tbsp cornmeal
- 3.5 oz breadcrumbs
- 5 tbsp cornstarch
- 0.25 cups of water
- 7 oz mozzarella cheese, cut into strips

1. Combine the water, cornmeal, cornstarch flour, garlic powder, and salt
2. Separately, combine the breadcrumbs, pepper, basil parsley, onion powder, and oregano
3. Dip the mozzarella sticks in the batter then cover in the breadcrumbs
4. Cook for 6 minutes at 390°F
5. Turn and cook for another 6 minutes

# 11.6. Picnic Scotch Eggs

| per serving | 407 Cal | 10g | 17g | 9g | 1g | 150 mg |

- 10 oz pork sausage, skins removed and mashed
- 2 eggs, beaten
- 6 boiled eggs, shells removed
- 1.7 oz flour
- 7 oz breadcrumbs

1. Divide the mashed sausage into six equal portions
2. Place an egg in the middle of each portion and close all the edges using your hands
3. Dip first in the flour, the egg, and the breadcrumbs
4. Cook in the air fryer at 390°F for 12 minutes

## 11.7. Cheesy Carrot Mushrooms

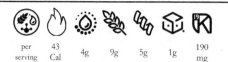

- 24 mushrooms
- 2 sliced of bacon, chopped
- 7 oz grated cheese
- 1 red pepper, sliced
- 1 onion, diced onion
- 1 carrot, diced
- 3.5 oz sour cream

1. Combine the pepper, carrot, onion and bacon in a pan and cook until soft, for around 5 minutes
2. Add the sour cream and cheese and combine until smooth
3. Stuff the mushrooms with the mixture and place in the air fryer
4. Cook at 350°F for 8 minutes

## 11.8. Chinese Spring Rolls

- 10 oz minced beef or pork
- 7 oz mixed vegetables
- 1 onion, diced
- 3 cloves of garlic, minced
- 5 oz dried rice noodles, soaked until soft
- 1 tsp sesame oil
- 1 tbsp vegetable oil
- 1 tsp soy sauce
- 1 pack of egg roll wrappers

1. Cook the minced beef/pork, onion, garlic, and vegetables for 6 minutes in a pan
2. Add the noodles and soy sauce and combine
3. Add some of the mixture to each egg roll wraps and fold in the middle section and corners. Roll and brush with the egg to seal the edges
4. Coat lightly in vegetable oil and place in the air fryer
5. Cos for 8 minutes at 360°F

## 11.9. Jalapeño & Cream Cheese Pops

| per serving | 190 Cal | 4g | 9g | 5g | 2g | 180 mg |

- 10 jalapeños, seeds removed and cut in half
- 5 oz breadcrumbs
- 1.7 oz parsley, chopped
- 3.5 oz cream cheese

1. Combine half the breadcrumbs with the cream cheese
2. Stir in the chopped parsley
3. Stuff the jalapeños with the mixture and sprinkle the rest of the breadcrumbs over the top
4. Cook in the air fryer for 6-8 minutes at 350°F

## 11.10. Fragrant Onion Pakora

| per serving | 185 Cal | 15g | 21g | 9g | 1g | 190 mg |

- 2 onions, sliced
- 7 oz gram flour
- 1 tbsp crushed coriander seeds
- 1 tsp chilli powder
- 1 tsp salt
- 0.24 tsp turmeric
- 0.25 tsp baking soda

1. Combine all ingredients until smooth
2. Use your hands to make ball shapes
3. Line the inside of the fryer basket with cooking foil
4. Arrange the pakoras inside and cook for 5 minutes at 390°F
5. Turn and cook for another 5 minutes

## 11.11 Bacon & Balsamic Sprouts

per serving | 100 Cal | 9g | 13g | 5g | 2g | 200 mg

- 2 tsp crumbled, cooked bacon
- 14oz halved Brussels sprouts
- 1 tbsp avocado oil
- 1 tsp balsamic vinegar
- Salt and pepper for seasoning

1. Mix the seasoning and oil together in a bowl
2. Add the sprouts and make sure they are covered completely in the mixture
3. Cook for 5 minutes at 347F
4. Shake well and continue to cook for a further 5 minutes
5. Serve with bacon and balsamic vinegar over the top

## 11.12 Cheesy, Garlic Asparagus

per serving | 296 Cal | 3g | 12g | 11g | 2g | 210 mg

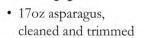

- 17oz asparagus, cleaned and trimmed
- 1 tbsp parmesan cheese, shredded
- 1 tsp olive oil
- 1 tsp garlic salt
- Salt and pepper for seasoning

1. Place the asparagus into the air fryer and drizzle a little oil over the top
2. Add the garlic salt and shredded parmesan, with as much seasoning as you prefer
3. Cook at 520F for 10 minutes

# 11.13 Spicy Corn on The Cob

| per serving | 196 Cal | 15g | 21g | 11g | 2g | 250 mg |

- 2 corn cobs, halved
- 2 tsp cheese, shredded
- 2.6oz mayonnaise
- 0.25 tsp chilli powder
- 1 tsp lime juice

1. Combine the lime juice, chilli powder, shredded cheese, and mayonnaise in a large bowl
2. Coat the corn in the mixture on all sides
3. Cook for 8 minutes at 392F

# 11.14 Parsley Snack Potatoes

| per serving | 100 Cal | 0.3g | 20g | 2g | 2g | 220 mg |

- 1 tbsp olive oil
- 17oz quartered baby potatoes
- 0.5 tsp parsley, dried
- 0.5 tsp garlic powder
- 1 tsp salt

1. Cook the minced beef/pork, onion, garlic, and vegetables for 6 minutes in a pan
2. Add the noodles and soy sauce and combine
3. Add some of the mixture to each egg roll wraps and fold in the middle section and corners. Roll and brush with the egg to seal the edges
4. Coat lightly in vegetable oil and place in the air fryer
5. Cos for 8 minutes at 360°F

# 11.15 Eggplant Snacks

| per serving | 200 Cal | 26g | 21g | 21g | 2g | 200 mg |

- 1 eggplant, sliced
- 2 eggs
- 3.5oz flour
- 7oz parmesan cheese, shredded
- 3.5oz breadcrumbs
- 0.5 tsp black pepper
- 0.5 tsp onion powder
- 1 tsp salt
- 0.5 tsp basil, dried
- 1 tsp Italian seasoning

1. Place the cheese, seasoning, and breadcrumbs in a bowl and mix with a fork
2. Take another bowl and add the flour
3. Add the egg to another bowl and beat
4. Take the eggplant and dip into the flour, eggs, and then the breadcrumb mixture
5. Cook in the air fryer at 365F for 8 minutes
6. Turn and cook for another 4 minutes

# 11.16 Snack Chickpeas

| per serving | 230 Cal | 8g | 30g | 6g | 3g | 250 mg |

- 1 can of drained chickpeas
- 0.5 cups of white vinegar
- 1 tbsp olive oil
- Salt for seasoning

1. Place the vinegar and chickpeas in a pan
2. Over a medium heat, combine and simmer for a few minutes
3. Allow to rest for 30 minutes, away from the heat
4. Place the chickpeas in the air fryer and cook at 375F for 4 minutes
5. Transfer to an ovenproof bowl
6. Add seasoning and the oil and combine
7. Place the bowl into the air fryer and cook for 4 minutes

2 | 5" | 25"

## 11.17 Zingy Shishito Peppers

| per serving | 256 Cal | 3g | 2g | 2.5g | 2g | 250 mg |

- 7oz shishito peppers
- 2 limes
- 2.6oz shredded cheese
- 0.5 tbsp avocado oil
- Salt and pepper for seasoning

1. Take a large bowl and add the oil, seasoning, and the peppers
2. Combine well
3. Place inside the fryer and cook for 10 minutes at 347F
4. Allow the cheese to melt on top of the peppers before serving

4 | 10" | 65"

## 11.18 Potatoes With Spinach

| per serving | 416 Cal | 23g | 28g | 26g | 2g | 280 mg |

- 2 tsp olive oil
- 1.7oz chopped spinach
- 2 potatoes
- 0.5 cups of yogurt
- 0.5 cups of whole milk
- Salt and pepper for seasoning

1. Take the potatoes and coat them slightly in oil
2. Place in the fryer and cook at 374F for 30 minutes
3. Turn over and cook for a further 30 minutes
4. Remove the middle of the potatoes using a spoon and mash with the yogurt and milk
5. Add the seasoning and spinach and mix until everything is incorporated
6. Place the mixture back inside the potato skins
7. Place back in the air fryer and cook at 320F for 5 minutes

# 11.19 Zucchini Snack Gratin

| | | | | | | |
|---|---|---|---|---|---|---|
| per serving | 183 Cal | 16g | 2g | 13g | 2g | 280 mg |

- 1 tbsp olive oil
- 2 zucchini, cut into slices
- 2 tbsp breadcrumbs
- 1 tbsp chopped parsley
- 4 tbsp shredded parmesan
- Salt and pepper for seasoning

1. Take a large bowl and combine all ingredients except the sliced zucchini
2. Arrange the sliced zucchini inside the air fryer and add the combined mixture on the top
3. Cook for 15 minutes at 350F

# 11.20 Airfryer Dill Pickles

| | | | | | | |
|---|---|---|---|---|---|---|
| per serving | 170 Cal | 16g | 15g | 2g | 2g | 250 mg |

- 1 jar of dill pickles, cut into slices
- 2 tbsp whole milk
- 1 egg
- 0.5 cups of mayonnaise
- 1.7oz flour
- 1.7oz cornmeal
- 2 tsp sriracha sauce
- 0.25 tsp paprika
- 0.5 tsp salt
- 0.5 tsp pepper
- 0.25 tsp garlic powder

1. Combine the sriracha sauce and mayonnaise and place to one side
2. Take another bowl and combine the milk and egg
3. In another bowl, add the rest of the ingredients, except for the dill pickles, and combine
4. Take the pickles and first dip into the egg and then the flour
5. Place in the air fryer and cook for 4 minutes at 392F

# CHAPTER 12
# MEAL PLAN

You'll now see that you can easily create delicious meals in your air fryer, but obviously it's not good to eat fried food for every single meal!

| | | | |
|---|---|---|---|
| Day 1 | Paprika Hash | Day 16 | Air Fryer Ravioli |
| Day 2 | Shrimp Pops | Day 17 | Pork & Marinara Sauce |
| Day 3 | Aubergine Parmesan | Day 18 | Salmon Burgers |
| Day 4 | Turkey in Mushroom Sauce | Day 19 | Lamb Kebabs |
| Day 5 | Pork Tenderloin in Dijon Mustard | Day 20 | Seasoned Belly Pork |
| Day 6 | Steak & Asparagus Cubes | Day 21 | Lasagne Taco Bake |
| Day 7 | Crab Stuffed Mushrooms | Day 22 | Cheese & Pasta Quiche |
| Day 8 | Cheese Tikka | Day 23 | Spicy Lamb Meatloaf |
| Day 9 | Beef Enchiladas | Day 24 | Air Fryer Pierogies |
| Day 10 | Zingy Shrimp | Day 25 | Chinese Spiced Pork |
| Day 11 | Stuffed Peppers With Beef | Day 26 | Mushroom Pasta |
| Day 12 | Potato Gratin | Day 27 | Beef Fried Rice |
| Day 13 | Zingy Lemon Chicken Wings | Day 28 | Turkey & Mushroom Burgers |
| Day 14 | Easy Breadcrumbed Fish | Day 29 | Chicken Thighs in Bacon |
| Day 15 | Coconut Asian Beef | Day 30 | Courgette Rolls |

# CHAPTER 13

# MEASUREMENTS

## 15.1 Volume Equivalents (Dry)

| Imperial | Mertic (Approximate) |
|---|---|
| 1/8 teaspoon | 0.5 mL |
| 1/4 teaspoon | 1 mL |
| 1/2 teaspoon | 2 mL |
| 3/4 teaspoon | 4 mL |
| 1 teaspoon | 5 mL |
| 1 tablespoon | 15 mL |
| 1/4 cup | 59 mL |
| 1/2 cup | 118 mL |
| 3/4 cup | 177 mL |
| 1 cup | 235 mL |
| 2 cups | 475 mL |
| 3 cups | 700 mL |
| 4 cups | 1 L |

## 15.2 Temperature Equivalents

| Fahrenheit (F) | Mertic (Approximate) |
|---|---|
| 225 ºF | 107 ºC |
| 250 ºF | 120 ºC |
| 275 ºF | 135 ºC |
| 300 ºF | 150 ºC |
| 325 ºF | 160 ºC |
| 350 ºF | 180 ºC |
| 375 ºF | 190 ºC |
| 400 ºF | 205 ºC |
| 425 ºF | 220 ºC |
| 450 ºF | 235 ºC |
| 475 ºF | 245 ºC |
| 500 ºF | 260 ºC |

## 15.3 Volume Equivalents (Liquid)

| US STANDARD | US STANDARD (Ounces) | Mertic (Approximate) |
|---|---|---|
| 2 tablespoons | 1 fl. oz. | 30 mL |
| 1/4 cup | 2 fl. oz. | 60 mL |
| 1/2 cup | 4 fl. oz. | 120 mL |
| 1 cup | 8 fl. oz. | 240 mL |
| 1 1/2 cup | 12 fl. oz. | 355 mL |
| 2 cups or 1 pint | 16 fl. oz. | 475 mL |
| 4 cups or 1 quart | 32 fl. oz. | 1 L |
| 1 gallon | 128 fl. oz. | 4 L |

## 15.4 Weight Equivalents

| US STANDARD | Mertic (Approximate) |
|---|---|
| 1 ounce | 28 g |
| 2 ounces | 57 g |
| 5 ounces | 142 g |
| 10 ounces | 284 g |
| 15 ounces | 425 g |
| 16 ounces (1 pound) | 455 g |
| 1.5 pounds | 680 g |
| 2 pounds | 907 g |

# CONCLUSION

The hope is that by this point, you're feeling completely inspired and you're ready to start creating delicious meals with your air fryer. You'll also be more confident because you know it's not as hard as you first thought.

All that's left to do is get started. These recipes give you a wide range of choices and you might be spoiled in terms of which one to opt for first. Take your time and follow all instructions. You'll quickly see how much potential your air fryer actually has.

Without the need to order takeaways or make high fat foods, you'll feel healthier and you'll probably feel far less sluggish as a result. You'll be able to make fantastic meals for all the family and even host dinner parties for your friends, using just your air fryer to wow them!

You can work your way through the recipes or you can choose a random recipe and start with that. Simply go with whatever option makes sense to you and whatever draws you. As long as you follow instructions, you'll have delicious food to serve and it will be on par with a restaurant in terms of crispiness and freshness.

All that's left for us to do is wish you luck. Gain confidence using your air fryer by familiarizing yourself with it beforehand. Then, there'll be no stopping you!

BONUS: Scanning the following QR code will take you to a web page where you can access 5 fantastic bonuses after leaving your email contact: Air Fryer Conversion Chart, Air Fryer Bucket List, Air Fryer Recipes To Cook First, Others Air Fryer Recipes, 1 mobile apps for iOS and Android.

LINK: https://BookHip.com/WLLCAPV

Printed in Great Britain
by Amazon

19536125R00054